INNOVATION THROUGH EDUCATION: BUILDING THE KNOWLEDGE ECONOMY IN THE MIDDLE EAST

Innovation through Education: Building the Knowledge Economy in the Middle East

Edited by Daniel Obst and Daniel Kirk

Fourth in a series of Global Education Research Reports

New York

IIE publications can be purchased at: www.iiebooks.org

The Institute of International Education
809 United Nations Plaza, New York, New York 10017

© 2010 by the Institute of International Education
All rights reserved. Published 2010
Printed in the United States of America
ISBN-13: 978-0-87206-325-9

Library of Congress Cataloging-in-Publication Data

Innovation through education : building the knowledge economy in the Middle East / edited by Daniel Obst and Daniel Kirk.
    p. cm. -- (Global education research reports ; v.4)
 ISBN 978-0-87206-325-9 (alk. paper)
1. Education, Higher--Middle East. 2. Educational innovations--Middle East. 3. International education--Middle East. 4. Student exchange--Middle East. 5. Knowledge, Sociology of--Middle East. I. Obst, Daniel. II. Kirk, Daniel N.
 LA1430.4.I45 2010
 378.56--dc22
                         2010016985

The views expressed in these chapters are solely those of the authors.
They do not necessarily represent the official positions of the
Institute of International Education or the AIFS Foundation.

Series editors:
Daniel Obst, Deputy Vice President for International Partnerships, IIE
Sharon Witherell, Director of Public Affairs, IIE
Shepherd Laughlin, Managing Editor

Cover image courtesy of Timon Maxey
Timon Maxey, "Dubai and Desert." Digital inkjet print. 7.5 x 10 inches. Map-accurate aerial view of Dubai and the desert with the Hatta Mountains at the bottom of the image.
Cover and text design: Pat Scully Design

TABLE OF CONTENTS

Appendices

FIGURES AND TABLES

FOREWORDS

By Allan E. Goodman

The Institute of International Education has been privileged to partner in the efforts of many countries and organizations to foster a knowledge economy. In recent years, IIE has undertaken a number of strategic initiatives in the Middle East, made possible through public and private investments in higher education and training in such countries as Saudi Arabia, the United Arab Emirates, Qatar, Jordan, and Egypt. Today, IIE delivers programs in the Middle East and North Africa region that reach over 7,000 students, scholars, and professionals each year. To cite a few examples of this work, last year IIE launched partnerships with the Qatar Foundation, NYU Abu Dhabi, the Carnegie Corporation of New York, and the Higher Colleges of Technology in Abu Dhabi to bring global talent to the region. Since May 2007, IIE has also worked with King Abdullah University of Science and Technology (KAUST) in Saudi Arabia to identify outstanding students globally to receive scholarships to pursue advanced degrees in science, technology and engineering.

This report reflects on the many steps that countries and organizations throughout the region are taking to create and retain talented people with the capacity to create new knowledge and the intercultural skills to put it to use. These range from major institutional initiatives like KAUST in Saudi Arabia and the El Hassan Science City in Jordan to academic exchange programs, like Fulbright and the Youth Exchange and Study (YES) programs, sponsored by the U.S. Department of State.

Despite the success of these programs, many challenges remain. One challenge is how to bring research and business together with academic initiatives to support the development of a sustainable, knowledge-based economy. The Qatar Science and Technology Park is one example of how this can be accomplished. With the support of Qatar's senior leadership, companies at the science park are forming research and education partnerships with the institutes in Education City. The QSTP's research-friendly facilities and a business environment that serves as an incubator for new technologies and start-up ventures attract world-leading corporate and academic research teams.

As Secretary of State Hillary Rodham Clinton noted during International Education Week, "education is an engine for change in all countries and for all people." The Middle East is a region where international education and training programs promise great potential to benefit not just the fortunate but also thousands of marginalized individuals whose talents are critical to their countries' development. As we continue to develop a global approach to education, the essays in this volume remind us that building a knowledge-based society is not confined to the classroom—it is a much larger project that links business, government, and academia, and transcends both borders and cultures.

Allan E. Goodman
President & CEO, Institute of International Education

BY WILLIAM L. GERTZ

We are once again delighted to partner with the Institute of International Education as we focus on educational exchange with the Middle East in this fourth installment of the Global Education Research Reports. While earlier reports in the series focused on the economic powerhouses of China and India, there is no more important region than the Middle East when it comes to the security of the United States and the future of our world.

Outbound educational participation for students from the Middle East is increasing dramatically, and the number of Middle Eastern middle and high schools students traveling to the U.S. and other nations for education is also rising. For example, our Summer Institute for the Gifted (SIG) program now has scores of participants from Saudi Arabia, Oman, Qatar, United Arab Emirates, and Bahrain. On this program, participants study at leading U.S. universities such as Princeton, UC Berkeley, Amherst, and UCLA, where they learn and work together with students from the U.S. and more than 30 other nations.

Since 2002, the AIFS Foundation has been involved with the Youth Exchange and Study Program (YES), a much admired high school exchange program bringing Muslim high school students to the United States. YES is operated under the auspices of the U.S. State Department, and has powerful supporters in Congress. The AIFS Foundation has helped to bring hundreds of Muslim students from the Middle East to live with American families and attend high school in the United States. AIFS has also noted growth in the number of young people from various Middle Eastern countries coming to work in the U.S. through our Au Pair in America and Camp America programs.

In contrast, overall participation in study abroad to the Middle East is extremely low: only 1.3 percent of U.S. college students who studied abroad in 2007/08 studied in the Middle East. Clearly, there is great potential for growth in this region. To this end, the Chairman of the American Institute For Foreign Study (AIFS), Sir Cyril Taylor, recently traveled to Syria to meet with education and government leaders to begin the process of creating a study abroad program at the University of Damascus. This university, which would welcome American students, certainly could be a catalyst for better relations.

AIFS is proud to be an active participant in helping to foster educational and cultural exchange with the Middle East and we look forward to providing even more educational opportunities in the future. We hope you will find these reports to be of interest and we thank the authors for their contributions to this project.

William L. Gertz
President & CEO, American Institute For Foreign Study (AIFS)
Trustee, AIFS Foundation

INTRODUCTION

JAMIL SALMI, TERTIARY EDUCATION COORDINATOR, WORLD BANK*

For decades, European scholars have dissented on whether the first medieval university was born in Oxford, Paris, or Bologna, ignoring in the course of their debate that the first university may in fact have preceded them all on the other side of the Mediterranean Sea. Indeed, the foundation of the University of Al-Karaouine in the Moroccan city of Fes and Al-Azhar in Egypt towards the end of the 10th century marked the beginning of a long tradition of teaching, cultural exchange, and scientific inquiry in the Arab world that endured well into the 20th century. For example, researchers and students from Iraq to Morocco recognized the University of Cairo as a beacon of scholarly excellence through the late 1960s.

Unfortunately, the emergence of Middle Eastern countries as independent nations in the 1950s and 1960s did not mark an acceleration of progress in education. In most countries in the region, the rapid quantitative expansion of education at all levels came at the cost of deteriorating quality. In its 2008 publication *The Road Not Traveled*, the World Bank documented the many challenges faced by education systems throughout the Arab world (World Bank, 2008). Middle Eastern countries are affected by challenging demographic factors, including a rapidly growing population and a youth bulge not seen elsewhere, in a context of increasingly limited fiscal resources. At the level of higher education, this has resulted in overcrowded and underequipped institutions, low-paid faculty, and rising graduate unemployment. It is therefore not surprising to observe that no Middle Eastern institution can be found in either the Shanghai Jiao Tong University Academic Ranking of World Universities or in the Times Higher Education Supplement international league tables.

The picture is not, however, entirely gloomy. In the midst of difficulties at the large public universities operating in the Middle East, many islands of scholarly excellence have been upheld by the determination of committed individuals. Universities in the West Bank and Gaza continue to function in spite of extreme economic and political constraints. Innovative institutions such as Al Akhawayn University in Morocco, the German-Jordanian University, or the Egypt-Japan University of Science and Technology have sprung up all over the region, following in the footsteps of

---

* The findings, interpretations, and conclusions expressed in this introduction are entirely those of the author and should not be attributed in any manner to the World Bank, the members of its Board of Executive Directors, or the countries they represent.

longstanding prestigious institutions such as the American University of Beirut and the American University in Cairo. The higher education landscape has seen even more widespread changes in the Gulf states and Saudi Arabia—the modernization of local universities, the establishment of prominent U.S. and European institutions, and ambitious projects to set up new universities or even entire university towns. The most emblematic illustration of this trend is perhaps the recently established King Abdullah University of Science and Technology, with its US$10 billion endowment, luxurious campus, international student body, and world-class research teams.

Against this background, this new publication on higher education in the Middle East, put together by the Institute of International Education (IIE) and the American Institute For Foreign Study (AIFS) Foundation, could not have arrived at a better time. Taking stock of positive developments in a part of the world that, more often than not, is portrayed in the news in a negative light, is a welcome undertaking. This report on higher education and the development of "knowledge societies" in the Middle East documents ongoing transformations of the higher education scene without hiding the difficulties faced by all participants in these global partnerships.

Focusing on the concept of the "knowledge society," the first chapter of the report, written by Daniel Kirk, introduces the challenges and opportunities related to modernization and transformation of higher education in the Middle East. The second chapter, by Spencer Witte, is an in-depth look at the ways different Gulf emirates have encouraged the development of foreign campuses, with a particular focus on Dubai and Abu Dhabi. The third chapter, by Robert G. Ayan Jr., looks at Jordan's strategies to develop and retain intellectual wealth, showing how these efforts are specifically matched to the needs of the kingdom.

Chapter four, written by Hana A. El-Ghali, Qianyi Chen, and John L. Yeager, reports on a study of strategic planning at institutions in non-Gulf countries in the region, with a focus on the issues and trends that guide their decisions. In chapter five, Haifa Reda Jamal Al Lail discusses the uplifting impact of internationalization in reducing the gender gap in higher education in the Middle East.

The next three chapters examine U.S.–Middle Eastern exchange. Sherifa Fayez and Dan Prinzing outline how youth exchange can help break cultural barriers, prejudice, and intolerance, with a specific focus on the Youth Exchange and Study (YES) program and efforts to expand exchange between the Middle East and the state of Idaho. In the next chapter, Jerome Bookin-Weiner and Ahmad Majdoubeh present overall trends in U.S. study abroad to the MENA region and discuss the potential for expanded exchange in the years to come. Finally, Norman J. Peterson and Yvonne M. Rudman offer an example of how to expand Arabic language education with limited resources—the U.S. Arabic Distance Learning Network, founded and based at Montana State University.

The final section of the report features three short pieces on IIE's activities related to the Middle East. The first is a summary of IIE's work in the region and the programs of the IIE MENA Regional Office based in Cairo, Egypt, written by Elizabeth

Khalifa and Daniel Obst. Second, Rajika Bhandari and Robert Gutierrez outline an ongoing pilot study aimed at elaborating a classification of higher education institutions in the Middle East, building on a similar mapping exercise recently completed in Europe. This kind of study will be particularly important in the Middle East, where nonuniversity institutions such as technical institutes and community colleges are not well regarded by society and not sufficiently integrated into the higher education system, even though they offer valuable opportunities for acquiring a relevant professional education that meets labor market needs. Finally, Patricia Chow and Shepherd Laughlin contribute a brief outline of historical trends in the number of Middle Eastern students studying at U.S. campuses, based on data from IIE's annual *Open Doors: Report on International Educational Exchange.*

This book is an important contribution to the debate on internationalization of higher education in the Middle East. Three key points are worth emphasizing by way of conclusion. First, to make a tertiary education institution global, it is not enough to set up an internationalization department responsible for organizing a few student and faculty exchanges. Taking full advantage of internationalization opportunities requires a comprehensive strategy that involves everyone on campus and permeates the curriculum—including the place and role of languages—as well as the institutional culture. Second, international partnerships can catalyze reform at tertiary education institutions in the Middle East as they consider issues such as governance and curricula. Finally, international linkages and partnerships can help counterbalance the negative reactions and perceptions that have emerged in the U.S. since September 11, 2001, which, as scholars including Jonathan R. Cole (2010) have noted, include visa restrictions for students from the Middle East, general mistrust against anything linked to the Arab and Islamic world, and selective harassment of U.S. scholars who conduct research on the Middle East.

I commend IIE and the AIFS Foundation for this new publication on the transformation of higher education in the Middle East. I hope that readers will find the report as informative and stimulating as I did.

REFERENCES

Cole, J. R. (2010). *The great American university: Its rise to pre-eminence, its indispensable national role, why it must be protected.* New York, NY: PublicAffairs Books.

World Bank. (2008). *The road not traveled: Education reform in the MENA region.* Washington, DC: The World Bank.

Chapter One

THE "KNOWLEDGE SOCIETY" IN THE MIDDLE EAST

DANIEL KIRK, FOUNDING PRESIDENT, GULF COMPARATIVE EDUCATION SOCIETY

Knowledge production and development is readily recognized as one of the main drivers of economic development, and those who are able to make best use of knowledge will also be those who perform most effectively within globalized economic structures (Aubert and & Reiffers, 2003). National and global political discourse is increasingly addressing the importance of developing "knowledge economies" and placing the production of knowledge societies at the forefront of national development policy. In terms of national development issues for central governments, the concern lies with attempting to understand what constitutes "knowledge," and once identified, how this can be assembled and delivered to local learners (Naidoo & Jamieson, 2005). For the purposes of this chapter, we view knowledge as sets of skills, understandings, expertise, and mastery of information, gained both through formal and informal education. Knowledge, and a definition of what constitutes a knowledge society, is a slippery concept, much discussed and debated, with defining elements often set by local and cultural ideology. So, with an awareness of the need to keep notions of many "knowledges" in mind, this chapter will explore how knowledge societies are developing in the Middle East.

Knowledge, transmitted traditionally through basic formal education, lifelong learning experiences, and informal educational settings, such as family and social environments, provides the basis for any fledgling knowledge-based society and economy. Building the knowledge capacity among the local citizenry is the most effective, and productive, way for the states of the Middle East to develop capacity and position themselves in relation to the global structures of knowledge production and dissemination that are increasingly contested among nations.

Governments across the Arab world are embracing development aims like those mentioned above, although progress continues to be slow, mired in regional and cultural considerations. However, those in the region understand that successful economies and societies must be well positioned and able to exploit knowledge to gain higher levels of productivity and competitive advantage. Arab societies have always placed great value on education and knowledge, along with the formal learning process (Herrera & Torres, 2006). For example, during the last millennium, the countries and peoples of what is now called the Middle East were advanced in terms of social, economic, and intellectual development. The knowledge production that began in the region swept through Europe and Asia, fueling a renaissance in learning for these regions.

There is a tendency to discuss the Middle East from a homogenous stance, as if the region were a single entity or even a nation-state, which fails to account for the heterogeneity of the countries in the region. As we discuss regional issues related to the creation of knowledge societies, we must acknowledge that local variations may stray from the norm across the region. We will address a few exceptional states and examples to allow for a more comprehensive understanding of the issue.

The Middle East is currently facing a raft of social, political, and economic challenges. The current fascination in the West with all things Middle Eastern is fueled, in part, by the media discourse surrounding high-profile regional conflicts, the scramble to secure oil resources, the global aspirations of a strengthening Iran, the global self-branding of Gulf city-states like Dubai, and the ongoing Israeli-Palestinian conflict. This means that regional governments are increasingly juxtaposed with Western systems and placed in opposition to the economic, social, and political norms of Europe and North America. This positioning in relation to, and often against, Western systems of governance takes place at several levels: Western governments place themselves in the role of "others"; some Middle Eastern leaders look to compete globally, often aspiring to embrace selected "Westernized" traits; and the populations in the region, especially the growing youth population in many countries, look West, while recognizing the need to retain their cultural identities.

The educational infrastructure and development of the Middle East is one aspect of social and national development that has increasingly been placed under the gaze of the global community. Western notions of education and the concept of building "knowledge societies" are gaining support in the region, although local obstacles continue to impede the growth of educational capacity, and are not easily overcome. Several high-profile, widely read reports published by the United Nations Development Programme have set in motion a period of regional introspection and a desire, at least in the rhetoric of policy makers, to improve local and regional knowledge production and capacity. In 2009, the *Arab Knowledge Report* proposed ways to fill numerous gaps that it identified in the educational capacity of the Arab world. This report came six years after the *Arab Human Development Report* (UNDP, 2003), which set out many of the problems faced by Arab states in developing education and access to wider notions of knowledge for the citizenry of the region. The clear link between knowledge and education as powerful drivers of economic growth, sustainability, and productivity became apparent to leaders and policy makers in the region. The report was also widely disseminated by nongovernmental agencies and academics, who touted it as evidence that social policy needed to be reviewed, particularly regarding access to education and the development of local educational capacity. Coupled to many of the issues that were stated in the UNDP report is an ongoing and prevalent perception in the region that Western educational credentials are the key to entry into the global knowledge economy, which in turn leads to higher status and reward for both individuals and nations (Doherty & Singh, 2005).

The *Arab Human Development Report* defines a knowledge-based society as "one where knowledge diffusion, production and application become the organizing principle in all aspects of human activity: culture, society, the economy, politics, and private life" (p. 2). Such an all-encompassing social, cultural, political, and economic role for education and the dissemination and production of knowledge is a lofty aim for any state or region. Human capital and high levels of educational attainment also play a crucial role in developing knowledge-based societies (Aubert & Reiffers, 2003).

In the Middle East, though, conditions are far from ideal for societies seeking to develop a knowledge base and build capacity. For example, Arab countries as a whole still have some of the lowest levels of research and development funding in the world (UNDP, 2009). Regional spending on research and development averaged 0.2 percent of GDP, compared to a global average of 1.7 percent (UNDP, 2009). The regional publication of books accounts for a mere 1.1 percent of the global total, and 15 percent of this output consists of religious texts (Greater Middle East Partnership, 2004). As a whole, the Arab world published fewer books than Turkey, and five times more books are published in Greek, spoken by just 11 million people (Greater Middle East Partnership, 2004), than in Arabic, spoken by an estimated 220 million people worldwide. Literacy rates are low in the region, with more than 40 percent of Arab women unable to read or write (Leyne, 2007).

These examples illustrate that the region, as a whole, is struggling to meet the necessary conditions for full and productive participation in the global knowledge economy, with Arab countries lagging behind other world regions in building knowledge-based economies and knowledge societies (Greater Middle East Partnership, 2004). As Starrett explains, "Muslim states have followed a different course to modernity [from the West], insisting explicitly that progress requires a centrally administered emphasis upon moral as well as economic development" (1998, p. 10).

There are, however, moves in some parts of the region to address the imbalances and obstacles that are faced across the wider Middle East. Saudi Arabia, a regional powerhouse, global economic force, and religious guide for the global Muslim community, has decided to invest heavily in education, the production of knowledge, and human development. According to recent data, the Saudi government spends 26 percent of nonmilitary GDP on education (Dunlop, 2010). When compared globally, this is an incredibly high percentage, and it is even more astounding in the regional context. This investment by the Saudi leadership is an attempt, in part, to counter growing criticism of the current educational system in the country and the wider region. Critics claim that education is not creating a productive and committed workforce that is ready to meet the demands of a global economy. Aware of an impending demographic time bomb (60 percent of the population is under the age of 20) and a projected doubling of the current population to 50 million by 2040, the government has prioritized education to meet national development goals and create an educated, knowledge-based workforce for the future. But in the eyes of many conservative Saudis, this has come at a price. Opening up the education system to the wider global environment and embracing economic globalization has required a reassessment of traditional social norms. This has led to a change in attitudes and expectations among a new, younger generation of educated Saudis.

Another example of a promising, high-profile attempt to develop the conditions needed to promote education and knowledge can be seen in Dubai, one of seven emirates that make up the United Arab Emirates. Dubai is accustomed to being in the global spotlight, and actively markets itself as a tourist destination, regional financial center, and the commercial heart of the Gulf Cooperation Council (GCC). Dubai is now positioning itself as the knowledge hub of the region (Kirk, 2009), with support from the ruler of Dubai, Sheikh Mohammed bin Rashid Al Maktoum, who recently donated $10 billion to establish a new education organization whose explicit goal is to raise education standards at all levels. According to Sheikh Mohammed, "There is a wide knowledge gap between us and the developed world in the West and in Asia. Our only choice is to bridge this gap as quickly as possible, because our age is defined by knowledge" (Leyne, 2007). Although the government of Dubai is moving toward enabling local infrastructure to promote knowledge acquisition, promotion, and diffusion, progress is slow, and has been further hampered by the global economic downturn, which has severely strained the budgets of publicly financed initiatives in the small emirate.

Despite such local efforts, the Middle East as a whole suffers from chronic underemployment and underutilized human potential, with the relatively wealthy Gulf states continuing to rely on imported labor, and poorer countries in the region experiencing a growing exodus as their youth seek higher salaries and educational opportunities abroad. With many of the youngest and brightest leaving the region for Western Europe and North America, the Arab world suffers from a chronic "knowledge deficit," creating a problem for states that want to train nationals to become efficient and effective members of local society (Al Shamsi, 2008), and by doing so, become less reliant on a transient, imported workforce. Part of this deficit stems from the education systems that exist in the region. Since education is generally provided free to the national population, the problem lies not with access to education, but with the quality and structure of government-funded education systems. Vocational and technical education, the teaching of basic sciences, and an overdependence on the social sciences means that new entrants into either the workforce or higher education may lack the skills and understanding needed to push forward knowledge production and research and development in the region. Education systems that focus on developing and promoting creative thinking, technological competence, language skills, and "global awareness" are few and far between in the Middle East. Yet it is precisely these elements of educational development that are needed for individual states to grow and fulfill their aspirations as members of a global knowledge-based economy and society. As the 2008 World Bank report *The Road Not Traveled* stated, education systems and structures in the Middle East need to be examined and a new approach to reform implemented if there is any chance of closing the gap between the educated few of the region and the internal and external labor demands that are increasingly compensating for the lack of national capacity.

Countries across the region, however, must address certain issues if they intend to bring the dream of knowledge-based societies to fruition. First, literacy rates remain low in the region, particularly among women, and this stunts knowledge growth and production. Because women play a crucial role in the workforce, addressing the low female literacy rates should be high on any list of priorities. Next, access to education, especially at the lower and secondary levels, is surprisingly low in many states, with students often completing the minimum number of years of compulsory schooling and departing formal education with few or no transferable skills and qualifications. The short duration of formal schooling results in an inadequately qualified workforce (Aubert & Reiffers, 2003), undermining the base necessary to produce higher-order thinkers who can move the knowledge society forward.

The Middle East remains a relatively wealthy region, which means that funding for education remains available, even in the poorer states, which benefit from a cultural tradition of sharing wealth and resources among the Arab nations. States such as Qatar, the United Arab Emirates, and Bahrain have developed dedicated education zones and areas that are promoting education and stimulating local research capacity and knowledge production. However, the current global economic downturn has undoubtedly had an impact on support, funding, and reform of education. Education has always been a soft target for policy makers in tough economic times, and this can be seen to some extent in the Middle East. There is also still a regional issue with "brain drain," which is proving difficult to reverse. As the region loses its brightest and most talented people, it continues to rely on foreign expertise, a situation that is unsustainable and incompatible with building local capacity.

Yet positive steps are being taken. There are localized efforts to expand local research and development capacity, such as the creation of the National Research Foundation in the United Arab Emirates. As societies begin to look beyond mere credentials and focus on developing critical thinking from an early age, highlighting and valuing education, and ensuring rigorous standards in education, the region will be well-positioned to move forward and take a leading role in contributing to the global knowledge economy.

REFERENCES

Al Shamsi, M. (2008). The imbalance in the population structure and its impact on the states of the region. In *Arabian Gulf security: Internal and external challenges* (pp. 389–447). Abu Dhabi, United Arab Emirates: Emirates Centre for Strategic Studies and Research.

Aubert, J., & Reiffers, J. (2003). *Knowledge economies in the Middle East and North Africa: Toward new development strategies.* Washington, DC: The World Bank.

Greater Middle East Partnership. (2004, February 13). *Al-Hayat.* Retrieved from http://www.albab.com/arab/docs/international/gmep2004.htm

Herrera, L., & Torres, C. A. (2006). *Cultures of Arab schooling: Critical ethnographies from Egypt.* Albany, NY: State University of New York.

Kirk, D. (in press). *Global reach, local need: The development and rise of the United Arab Emirates higher education sector.* Abu Dhabi, United Arab Emirates: Emirates Centre for Strategic Studies and Research.

Leyne, J. (2007, May 19). Dubai ruler in vast charity gift. *BBC News Online.* Retrieved from http://news.bbc.co.uk/2/hi/middle_east/6672923.stm

Dunlop, G. (Director). (2010, February 13). *Saudi goes to market* [Television documentary]. London, United Kingdom: BBC World News.

Starrett, G. (1998). *Putting Islam to work: Education, politics, and religious transformation in Egypt.* Berkeley, CA: University of California Press.

United Nations Development Programme. (2003). *Arab human development report 2003: Building a knowledge society.* New York, NY: United Nations Development Programme.

United Nations Development Programme. (2009). *Arab knowledge report 2009: Towards productive intercommunication for knowledge.* New York, NY: United Nations Development Programme.

World Bank. (2008). The road not traveled: Education reform in the Middle East and North Africa. Washington, DC: World Bank.

Chapter Two

DIFFERENT EMIRATES, DIFFERENT MODELS: CREATING GLOBAL INSTITUTIONS IN THE GULF STATES

SPENCER WITTE, POLICY ANALYST AND RESEARCHER, ISHTIRAK

We can bring people from Syria, from Pakistan, from Iran, from everywhere to give them an American education. It's the American global dream that can only happen in Dubai because it's such a global city.

> Dr. Abdullah Al Karam, Former CEO, Dubai Knowledge Village
> (Bardsley, "Tuition fees checked by universities' expansion," 2008)

The concern is the quality and many people look at education as a business... In the end we will be left with only the good institutions—you can't compare institutions like the Sorbonne and NYU with the others.

> Abdullah al-Khanbashi, Vice Chancellor,
> United Arab Emirates University
> Personal communication, 21 September 2008

Currently, the education system of the United Arab Emirates consists of more than 60 public and private colleges and universities intended to meet the needs of just over five million people. Almost all of its systemic expansion has taken place in the last decade, and much more expansion has been promised. For example, Warren Fox, director of higher education at the Dubai Knowledge and Human Development Authority (KHDA), has recommended quadrupling the number of graduates from Dubai's private universities in the next ten years (Mills, "Emirates look to the West for prestige," 2008). The Emirate of Abu Dhabi has pursued ambitious partnerships with the likes of Paris-Sorbonne University and New York University. The Emirate of Ras al-Khaimah, while smaller and shorter on resources, announced a $1 billion scheme for the development of its own free zone for education. If this plan is carried out, it will involve as many as 15 foreign institutions and accommodate 38,000 students (Bardsley, "Economy needs more graduates," 2008). And, according to the 2007

IIE/AIFS Foundation Global Education Research Reports
INNOVATION THROUGH EDUCATION: BUILDING THE KNOWLEDGE ECONOMY IN THE MIDDLE EAST

7

strategic plan produced by the Ministry of Higher Education and Scientific Research (MOHESR), public institutions can expect an additional 20,000 Emirati enrollments by 2020 (UAE MOHESR, 2007).

This chapter seeks to contextualize the arrival and proliferation of foreign degree-granting branch campuses in this complex and dynamic policy environment. It would be a mistake, however, to examine the UAE tertiary system in the aggregate. The emirates are separate entities pursuing largely separate higher education strategies. To demonstrate this crucial point, special attention will be given to recent agreements linking two of America's strongest universities with the two largest emirates, Dubai and Abu Dhabi. There is much to learn from each case. Michigan State University-Dubai (MSU-Dubai) is largely vocational in emphasis and operates on a self-sustaining financial model. New York University Abu Dhabi (NYU Abu Dhabi) will be a full liberal arts research university when it opens in fall 2010. It will draw on comprehensive federal funding toward its goal of enrolling more than 2,000 students. This article will also discuss how these efforts in the UAE compare to another innovative Gulf-state model, Qatar's Education City.

The terms of each arrangement are highly revelatory of the divergent economic and social aims of Dubai and Abu Dhabi. Branch campuses are an important window into understanding the dispositions of each emirate toward their respective expatriate populations. The speed with which tertiary institutions are being introduced—as well as the range of degrees on offer—is also suggestive. It mirrors the historical disparities in the pace and nature of development between Dubai and Abu Dhabi. And lastly, their choice in partnership models reflects different economic and social priorities arising from incongruent levels of wealth.

Before weighing the recent histories of the two emirates against their present-day higher education strategies, it is necessary to briefly examine the challenges that the UAE has faced in its provision of public higher education. Autonomy at the level of the individual emirates allows for policy responses that are consistent with the respective histories of Dubai and Abu Dhabi and, typically, inconsistent with one another.

Challenges to Public Higher Education Provision

The UAE's public tertiary institutions consist of the United Arab Emirates University (UAEU; founded in 1977), the more vocationally oriented Higher Colleges of Technology (HCT; 16 campuses, the first of which was founded in 1988), and Zayed University (ZU; initially founded as a women's university in 1998). From the start, the UAE's public higher education system adopted a Western orientation (Peck, 1986, p. 76), and this has only become more noticeable over time. Zayed's curriculum was designed to conform closely to the U.S. model (Halloran, 1999, p. 330) and it recently received accreditation from an American agency.[1] UAEU is also pursuing American accreditation (Mills, "Emirates look to the West for prestige," 2008). Expatriates predominate in the education ministries and also occupy key administrative positions within the public tertiary institutions.[2] Today, 35,000 students are spread between UAEU, HCT, and ZU (UAE MOHESR, 2007, p. 12).

Despite growing enrollment, federal spending on higher education remained dangerously stagnant until very recently. ZU, for instance, experienced a 52 percent increase in students over a six-year period, but nonetheless worked with a fixed budget in that time (UAE National Media Council, 2009, p. 229). Even with considerable concurrent nominal GDP growth, public expenditure on education as a percentage of UAE GDP stood at just 1.6 percent in 2002 (World Bank, 2008, p. 312).[3] However belated, an infusion of federal money and a reworked funding formula that adjusts institutional budgets according to student numbers was welcome news for the public tertiary system in the 2009–2010 academic year.

There can be little doubt that the UAE public tertiary system remains overburdened. Emirati nationals are promised free schooling through the university level, and the maintenance of separate gender-segregated facilities in public institutions adds substantially to costs (Bristol-Ryhs, 2008, p. 101). A 2007 government memo estimated that as many as 3,000 qualified applicants to the HCT had to be turned away because of concerns over inadequate space and diminished quality (Davidson, 2008a, p. 208). There is also a widely held view that the public system has underperformed, creating neither value-added research nor needed links to the private sector. As Walters, Kadragic, and Walters conclude succinctly, "…the typical 'tier II' university in the United States has more patents issued to its faculty in a year than do all citizens and residents of the UAE combined" (2006, p. 4).

In part because of the traditional availability of public-sector jobs and also the potential for steady revenue through the *kafil* system, Emirati men are underrepresented in higher education. The *kafil* system mandates that at least 51 percent of all UAE-based companies be nationally owned. This arrangement makes it possible for a national partner, or sponsor, to earn a lucrative sum by simply signing on to a foreign-based business venture. In 2003, over half of all male students who were approved for admission to federal universities failed to show up for registration, and men overall make up just 28 percent of enrollment in public higher education (Fox, 2008, p. 120–121).

Male graduates are entering the job market underqualified and with unrealistic expectations for employment. The public sector has reached a point of saturation and simply can no longer accommodate these graduates. More than 19,000 nationals are projected to enter the job market in 2010. Considering that Tanmia, a federal organization responsible for assisting Emiratis toward occupational placement, was only able to place just over 12 percent of its 6,563 job-seekers in 2003, this number becomes especially daunting (Nicks-McCaleb, 2005, p. 327).

In marked contrast, the UAE's private sector has shown considerable recent growth, accounting for 52.1 percent of available jobs. Emiratis make up between 15 and 20 percent of the total population, but just 13,000 out of 3 million total workers in the private sector. It is estimated that by 2020, Emiratis will make up less than 4 percent of the total workforce (UAE National Media Council, 2009, p. 210). To help redress this imbalance, the UAE has enacted long-running labor nationalization policies, often collectively called "Emiratization." But estimates suggest that expatriates now willingly assume salaries 135 percent lower than similarly qualified nationals (Davidson, 2008a, p. 207). Although Emiratization policies continue, to date they have largely failed. Expatriates are widely presumed to be better trained, harder working, more cost effective and also easier to fire.

At the emirate level, policymakers have demonstrated a clear desire to better direct their own educational policies even as a coordinated strategic planning at the federal level is taking form. In 2005, Dubai and Abu Dhabi created separate education policymaking bodies, the Abu Dhabi Education Council (ADEC) and the Dubai Education Council (DEC). The initiatives of the latter have since been subsumed by the Dubai Knowledge and Human Development Authority (KHDA). Disparate emirate-level strategies make establishing a consistent and effective federal policy even more challenging. We now turn our attention to the level of the individual emirates.

Dubai in Recent History: Open Arms and Opportunism

At the time of Britain's announced withdrawal from the present-day UAE in 1968, the local population stood at a mere 180,000 (Fenelon, 1973, p. 8). By the mid-1970s, the number had grown to 658,000 and included a non-national population of 456,000 (Birks, 1988, p. 135). This imbalance was perceived differently across the emirates. For decision makers in Abu Dhabi it was nothing short of disconcerting, and anxiety soon became manifest in federal policy. The development plan for 1977–1979 recommended a more restrictive immigration policy. Abu Dhabi articulated a goal of limiting the importation of additional manpower over the three-year span to between 191,000 and 244,000, and also recommended introducing further reductions to the provision of inter-emirate transit visas (Sakr, 1980, p. 181).

For policy makers in Dubai, the restrictions, and not the unevenness of the population, served as the real source of anxiety. Dubai has a long history of welcoming considerable foreign expertise and commerce. A decade into the 1900s, Dubai was already more diverse than any of the neighboring sheikhdoms. By then, Kuwaiti and Bahraini Arabs, Persians, Baluchis, and Indians all held significant tracts of land (Heard-Bey, 1982, p. 242). By and large, however, these communities did not mix. Instead, entrepreneurs and private companies were encouraged to provide services to meet the separate needs of each community. Prominent examples of this pertaining to education include a Shah-established Iranian school in Dubai and several other schools established by wealthy Indian merchants in the years just before the founding of the federation (Davidson, 2008b, p. 640).

Crucially, the British East India Steam Navigation Company resolved to make Dubai a regular port of call in 1904. Davidson concludes that the decision confirmed "Dubai's position as the main distribution centre for goods along the whole littoral from Qatar to Ras al-Khaimah" (2008a, p. 68). Dubai has since aggressively sought to maintain and further its reputation as the most active and welcoming center of trade in the region.

Therefore, by the time Dubai began exporting oil in 1969, it was already benefiting from an extensive tradition of private enterprise. A substantial part of the sheikhdom's workforce was engaged in trade, some 36 percent of the population (Fenelon, 1973). Dubai's supply of hydrocarbons, always modest relative to Abu Dhabi's, has been used in support of a policy of frantic industrialization characterized by high-risk initiatives. Oil was never the projected centerpiece of the local economy.

In fact, by 2005, only 5 percent of the emirate's GDP owed to hydrocarbons, whereas the services sector in that same year accounted for 74 percent (UAE MOHESR, 2007, p. 19). A series of bold ventures—the development of Dubai's airport, Port Rashid, and the Jebel Ali Free Zone all serve as examples—have aimed to solidify Dubai's position as the region's premier center for trade. Yet, they have also required large amounts of labor. The port at Jebel Ali, for example, was estimated to require 400,000 additional laborers (Sakr, 1980, p. 181). It should be emphasized that where Abu Dhabi has generally leaned on smaller influxes of culturally similar Arab and Pakistani workers, Dubai's larger, more diverse expatriate population reflects a more business-minded expedience. Despite the fact that nationals are now estimated to be a mere 4 percent of the population (Davidson, 2008a, p. 190), the Dubai Strategic Plan 2015 projects a need for 882,000 additional workers in order to achieve the emirate's broader economic goals (UAE MOHESR, 2007, p. 23).

Both Dubai's historically laissez-faire commercial approach and the centrality of expatriate labor to rapid economic diversification are reflected in the emirate's present-day higher education system. The gathering of branch campuses within free zones explicitly caters to the needs of separate expatriate communities. It corresponds to foreign direct investment in other sectors. And it aims to attract more talent to Dubai while keeping the children of expatriates—who would otherwise have to leave the UAE between the ages of 18 and 21 because of federal labor laws—present and making vital contributions to the local economy.

Dubai's network of private tertiary institutions inspires high levels of competition for potential student enrollment. The success of branch campuses is contingent on adequate enrollment to generate enough income to pay rent on privately owned, free-zone land. If enrollment continues, so do payments. As a partial product of this arrangement, the program and degree offerings of branch campuses are often vocational and preprofessional in nature. They are meant to directly address the changing needs of the diversifying labor market while serving as attractive options for job seekers.

Higher Education in Dubai: Dubai Knowledge Village and the Free Market

Between 1993 and 2005, Dubai's population more than doubled from 600,000 to over 1.3 million. In part to accommodate the needs of exploding demographics, private higher education providers have become predominant in the emirate. The majority of this systemic expansion has occurred through the development of Dubai Knowledge Village (DKV) and its more ambitious offshoot, Dubai International Academic City (DIAC).

Dubai Knowledge Village was founded in 2002. It is owned and operated by TECOM Investments, a subsidiary of the massive (and now financially troubled) Dubai Holding. TECOM also oversees the development of Dubai Internet City and Dubai Media City—which are not wholly separate projects. As Al Karam and Ashencaen explain, "Dubai Knowledge Village is deeply committed to providing practical programmes to compliment the knowledge economy. To serve the ICT hub; Dubai Internet city, many KV degree programmes are weighted towards IT, science and business management. Media courses are offered to support the emerging media industry centered at Dubai Media City" (2004, p. 6). In this way, the synergies between higher education and private industry—considered so vital in the West but largely absent in the Arab world—take form. But such links also potentially create substantial monetary benefit to the other major TECOM initiatives and, in so doing, attract future business and settlement in the free zones.

DKV is situated near the Dubai Technology and Media Free Zone on 1 million square feet of land. Its institutions are promised 100 percent tax-free repatriation of assets and profits as well as ready-made buildings and facilities from which to operate. In return, TECOM leases the land and the buildings and effectively collects rent (Krieger, "An academic building boom transforms the Persian Gulf," 2008). This sort of arrangement allows institutions new to the free zone to begin operating very soon after arrival. For an emirate that recently articulated a goal of sustaining real GDP growth at 11 percent per annum over a ten-year span (UAE MOHESR, 2007, p. 21), a more deliberate tempo borders on unacceptability. Brendan Mullan, executive director of Michigan State University Dubai, described the speed at which he was expected to carry out a similar arrangement in DIAC: "In January it was me and the laptop. Eight months later, I have 33,000 square feet, a faculty and staff of 28 people and I have students taking classes" (personal communication, September 16, 2008).

But which providers have been attracted to DKV, and, in turn, what student demographic is it catering to? DKV has been unambiguous about its desire to attract expatriate students to the UAE and then retain them after they graduate. Quite obviously, this strategy is in contradiction to federal Emiratization policies, but is also very much consistent with Dubai's traditional openness to diverse populations contributing to strong economic growth. N. Janardhan, program manager at the Gulf Research Center, explains, "Dubai realized that there is a certain constituency that can be tapped for further economic development as part of its diversification.

With Knowledge Village, many parents began to think that rather than sending kids back home, they might as well keep them here" (personal communication, September 20, 2008).

Within a year of its founding, DKV had welcomed 15 regional and international universities from nine countries. This list included institutions from Australia, India, Iran, and Pakistan. In the case of Iran, Islamic Azad University opened a Dubai branch, granting access to the 450,000 Iranian citizens located in the emirates. It is a wealthy group that as recently as 2007 held between $20 to $200 billion of Dubai's assets (Fattah and El Sawy, "Young Iranians follow dreams to Dubai," 2005). TECOM perceptively saw an opportunity to cater to an explicitly national educational niche.

Yet this approach clearly raises issues. How do so many curricula, languages, and competing pedagogical philosophies operate within one system? Furthermore, many DKV institutions are of second-tier quality, and because of their location inside of a free zone, they do not have to apply for licensing from the Ministry of Higher Education and Scientific Research. In fact, part of the appeal of establishing a branch campus in Dubai is a promise that the emirate will have no say in the workings of the institution. Instead, a separate group, the University Quality Assurance International Board, was launched in 2008 by the Dubai Knowledge and Human Development Authority to vet institutions and ensure that the quality of education offered at the home campus is replicated in Dubai's free zones. Several institutions in DKV persist without licensing or accreditation from the Ministry's Commission for Academic Accreditation; their graduates will consequently be disallowed from obtaining jobs in the public sector (Bardsley, "University warns of overexpansion," 2008).

Dubai Knowledge Village has also drawn criticism for the quality of experience it can provide its students. It has been compared to a "shopping mall of universities" and has already run out of space. It never attempted to provide students and faculty with cutting-edge laboratories, sporting venues, or even student housing (Krieger, "An academic building boom transforms the Persian Gulf," 2008). And, as evidenced by the closing of the Southern Queensland University-Dubai in 2005, partnerships with TECOM have occasionally lacked the strength and communication necessary to create sustainable operations. Incredibly, Southern Queensland was brought to DKV without the knowledge of the University's president (Cohen, "Australian university closes campus in United Arab Emirates in dispute with government," 2005). DKV's other institutions were left unhappy when the cost of rent increased 30 percent in the course of 2005 (McMurtrie, "Overseas programs increasingly sharing risk with host countries," 2006).

Perhaps it is hardly surprising that first-rate American institutions proved reluctant to become involved in DKV. Several early potential collaborations fell through, including a near agreement with Boston University, and later NYU. In the case of NYU, its president, John Sexton, requested all future construction and operating costs in addition to a $50 million one-time gift (Lewin, "U.S. universities rush to set up outposts abroad," 2008). This deal would have represented a significant departure from the Dubai model, establishing a new precedent the emirate could not afford.

Michigan State University Dubai and the Development of DIAC

For administrators at Michigan State University, the self-sustaining financial model made sense. In principle, they supported a Gulf-based branch campus, but articulated concern that a project funded by foreign investors might impinge on the autonomy needed to shape academic policy.

This was not an issue in Dubai. Over the course of 2007, administrators met several times with officials from the KHDA and henceforth agreed to become part of Dubai International Academic City (DIAC). DIAC signals a shift in Dubai strategy toward higher quality. And Michigan State—a major American research university consistently ranked in the top 100 in the world—is meant to be central to this redirection. To begin with, DIAC encompasses a significantly larger land area—25 million square feet at an estimated cost of $3.27 billion (Krieger, "Dubai aiming to be an academic hub, strikes a deal with Michigan State," 2007).

The DKV plot will continue to maintain its collection of mostly second-tier vocational and technical schools, whereas DIAC, announced in April 2005 and inaugurated in late 2006, is supposed to attract higher quality institutions. Of the 54 foreign universities that applied for a place in DIAC in 2007, only five were approved (Bardsley, "No free zone for universities in capital," 2008). In contrast to the basic provisions of DKV, TECOM promised DIAC's participating institutions educational and community infrastructure, including residence halls, R&D labs, a sports stadium, and entertainment and retail outlets.

DIAC proved an attractive destination for Michigan State on several levels. TECOM consented to the extension of a generous credit line that would help to cover start-up costs. In the coming years, revenue from tuition could allow MSU to pay back this loan. MSU is ensured total academic autonomy as well as the opportunity to fulfill its mission of providing the same quality of education as is delivered at the home campus in East Lansing. Dubai was singled out as a lively, cosmopolitan location, as a "magnet for the region's youth" (Brendan Mullan, personal communication, September 16, 2008).

The scope of the project is small, but early enrollment numbers are nonetheless disappointing (a mere 106 undergraduates were enrolled at the start of the 2009–2010 academic year). It is hoped that after four years, as many as 750 to 1,000 will enroll. To these ends, a foundation year is being used to qualify students and boost numbers. MSU Dubai also took the unusual step of offering half-price tuition for incoming transfer students. Yet, out of 40 applications to the home campus, only 20 students were admitted (Bardsley, "University's half-price tuition scheme gets disappointing pass rate," 2010).

MSU Dubai endeavored to line up strong course offerings with subjects suited to Dubai's stated needs. Administrators met with local constituencies from the media, construction, and computing industries and six undergraduate programs were established: business administration, child and youth development, computer engineering, construction project management, early childhood education, and media management and research. Three master's programs are offered, including degrees in human resources and labor relations. Enrolled undergraduates must also complete a regimen of core liberal arts courses in line with home-campus graduation requirements.

Abu Dhabi in Recent History: The Cautious Use of Wealth

Abu Dhabi's development contrasts markedly with that of Dubai. Pearling continued to serve as the economy's predominant industry in the immediate post–World War II era. At that time, it accounted for a full 85 percent of the sheikhdom's total national income (Shihab, 2001, p. 260). With this longtime, singular economic focus, Abu Dhabi has not had the kind of history of private enterprise that has defined Dubai. Indeed, Fenelon refers to Abu Dhabi in the pre-oil era as "…an economic backwater with few trading or other contacts with the outer world" (1973, p. 65).

In fact, from 1928–1966 Abu Dhabi was subjected to particularly inward-looking leadership under Sheikh Shakhbut ibn Sultan Al Nahyan. Large commercial quantities of oil were found in Abu Dhabi in 1959, some seven years before a much more modest discovery was made in neighboring Dubai. Shakhbut was reputedly concerned for the demographic composition of Abu Dhabi. Rapid development had already transformed Kuwait, and Shakhbut was wary of bringing similar changes to his sheikhdom. He erected trade barriers, and in 1961 went so far as to prohibit any new construction in Abu Dhabi (Davidson, 2007, p. 35). Foreign merchants, including Arabs, were often kept from conducting business altogether (Davidson, 2008b, p. 640).

The consequences of these measures are hardly surprising: Abu Dhabi remained grossly underdeveloped and the maturation of local private business was stunted. In fact, Davidson contends that Abu Dhabi's business community was "irrevocably weakened" (2007, p. 35) when many of the sheikhdom's most prominent merchants continued to relocate to Dubai's more auspicious commercial environment well into the 1960s.

Abu Dhabi was also late in developing a formal school structure. A substantial amount of educational assistance to the Gulf was directed through the Kuwaiti Gulf Permanent Assistance Committee, but this too was rejected by Shakhbut as a manifestation of foreign assistance. When he finally agreed to the creation of two schools in 1961, both were hamstrung with unusually parochial curricular requirements, including a stipulation that outlawed the teaching of any other history apart from Abu Dhabi's (Davidson, 2008c, p. 34).

Shakhbut ceded power in 1966 to his brother Sheikh Zayed bin Sultan Al Nahayan in a bloodless coup. Development proceeded, but did not parallel the pace of industrialization in Dubai. It did not have to. Abu Dhabi's oil reserves are massive—today the emirate holds 16 percent of OPEC's total proven resources and over 90 percent of the UAE's total supply. If one were to calculate the GDP per capita through proven oil reserves alone, the number would stand at a staggering $17 million per Abu Dhabi national (Davidson, 2007, p. 37). Such wealth has inspired a purposefully measured approach. The "Plan Abu Dhabi 2030," published in 2007, is representative. Under a heading titled "sustainability," it explains "Oil has brought considerable wealth to the city, but it is a finite resource. Abu Dhabi's future lies in the ability to cautiously use existing wealth.... Resource efficiency is vital" (Urban Planning Council, 2007, p. 11).

It is estimated that UAE oil reserves will last more than 120 years. Still, as a capital-intensive industry, the oil sector manages to employ only 1.6 percent of the federation's workforce (Shihab, 2001, p. 252). Job creation should therefore be seen as a major motivating factor in Abu Dhabi's decision to diversify its economy. And yet, Abu Dhabi exhibits a sustained awareness of a central fact: major industrialization necessitates the importation of more foreign labor. Abu Dhabi's leadership has, on occasion, expressed an unequivocal uneasiness about the national-expatriate population imbalance. For example, Sheikh Zayed bin Sultan Al-Nahyan, former President of the UAE, stated that a majority expatriate population posed, "a grave problem which threatens the stability of our society and the prospects for future generations" (Janardhan, 2006, p. 8).

Accordingly, Abu Dhabi has sought an economic strategy reliant on heavy industry and overseas investments largely channeled through the Abu Dhabi Investment Authority (ADIA). Abu Dhabi attracts only 9 percent of the UAE's foreign direct investment (Davidson, 2007, p. 43). This strategy allows for a more measured orientation to the issue of additional labor importation.

Similarly, Abu Dhabi's incredible wealth has fostered an approach to education that is less concerned with the immediate needs of the local economy and more reflective of a longer process. Encouraging an appreciation for culture and the liberal arts are twin aims. Tellingly, the emirate has chosen to allow for the establishment of indigenous private institutions while inviting partnership with a select few foreign institutions, both of elite stature. This strategy is historically consistent with Abu Dhabi's vision of careful diversification. It also acts to supplement the emirate's emerging luxury tourism sector.

Higher Education in Abu Dhabi: Ambitious Conservatism and NYU Abu Dhabi

Relative to Dubai, Abu Dhabi's higher education strategy appears cautious. As Peter Heath, a longtime educator in the Arab world and the current chancellor of the American University of Sharjah, explains, "Abu Dhabi looks at Dubai and asks, is this really the model we want to use? Abu Dhabi has the advantage of having enough resources, they've become more hesitant more conservative in where they're going because, actually, they don't have to go anywhere" (Peter Heath, personal communication, September 18, 2008).

In 2007 the Abu Dhabi Education Council (ADEC) turned away the applications of 30 foreign universities that offered to open in the emirate. In so doing, it implicitly rejected the Dubai model and that emirate's free-zone strategy (Bardsley, "No free zone for universities in capital," 2008). Yet, a more measured approach should not be interpreted to mean that Abu Dhabi is standing still—hardly so. While the emirate has been demonstrably selective in its recruitment of foreign branch campuses, its chosen partnerships have also been extremely ambitious and high profile. The Paris-Sorbonne University Abu Dhabi (2006) and New York University Abu Dhabi (set to open in fall of 2010) are not meant to plug immediate gaps in job market needs, but are instead designed to offer world-class education opportunities "previously only available to students overseas" (UAE Executive Council, 2007, p. 32). The two universities will make up the emirate's elite higher education sector, but are intended to serve other functions as well. The addition of the Sorbonne and NYU complement Abu Dhabi's emerging tourism sector and advance an image of the emirate as a global cultural hub.

Abu Dhabi's hydrocarbon sector does not have the capacity to employ large numbers of people. The emirate's tourism sector, however, has shown tremendous promise. Estimates suggest that tourism contributed as much as 7.6 percent of all employment in Abu Dhabi in 2005. More importantly, GDP from tourism increased 62 percent from 2001–2006, suggesting high growth potential. According to the 2007–2008 Abu Dhabi Executive Council Policy Agenda "...the Emirate is embarking on an ambitious strategy to attract 3 million visitors per year by 2015.... Every aspect of the Emirate's tourism strategy and its implementation works toward the reputation of Abu Dhabi as an exclusive, high-end tourist destination...the Abu Dhabi tourism strategy will contribute to the international reputation of the Emirate, create significant business opportunities and stimulate the growth of an empowered private sector and the creation of a sustainable knowledge-based economy" (UAE Executive Council, 2007, p. 18).

The Sorbonne agreed to establish an Abu Dhabi branch campus in May 2006. Diverging from the mostly vocational options on offer in DKV, the Paris-Sorbonne University Abu Dhabi was contracted to provide both undergraduate and graduate degrees in social sciences, humanities, and the fine arts. It is wholly owned by ADEC, which pays all of the university's expenses.

Several other high-profile agreements coincided with the Sorbonne's arrival. In July 2006, a Memorandum of Understanding was signed with the Guggenheim Foundation to create a world-class modern art museum. And in March 2007, a 30-year contract was finalized for the establishment of the Louvre Abu Dhabi museum. For Abu Dhabi, these initiatives have had the effect of signaling a greater openness to the outside world while significantly raising consumer consciousness of the emirate as a potential high-end destination.

These moves are unambiguously bold. Yet consistent with its history, Abu Dhabi continues to wrestle with the same dilemma: to what extent can the emirate open itself without losing its traditional culture and heritage? Policymakers in Abu Dhabi believe they have crafted a strategy that will allow for a balanced answer to this question. The emirate has also recently founded the Abu Dhabi Authority for Culture and Heritage (ADACH) and declared 2008 to be "The Year of National Identity." The Abu Dhabi Executive Council Policy Agenda explains, "An effective policy for the conservation and enhancement of culture and heritage in Abu Dhabi will contribute to: 1) The education of current and future generations. 2) The creation of a unique tourist offering. 3) Ensuring that economic growth and diversification results in the wider dissemination rather than the diminishment of the Emirate's rich cultural heritage" (UAE Executive Council, 2007, p. 40).

The establishment of NYU Abu Dhabi, announced in October 2007, is a component of this balancing act. The construction of the Guggenheim Abu Dhabi, the Louvre Abu Dhabi, and NYU Abu Dhabi are all overseen by the Tourism Development and Investment Company (TDIC), a government-established organization responsible for carrying out large-scale projects identified by the Abu Dhabi Tourism Authority (ADTA). All three initiatives will be located on Saadiyat Island, a proposed cultural district with an estimated development cost of $28 billion. The island was a major draw for NYU decision makers. As Philip Kennedy, a standing faculty member and part of a small NYU Abu Dhabi planning team explained, "The [NYU] administration is very happy about the location because of the kind of prestige it lends to the project.... They will design what we hope will tie into a thriving, surrounding cultural ambiance" (Philip Kennedy, personal communication, September 21, 2008).

Once completed, the NYU Abu Dhabi campus will feature classrooms, libraries, laboratories, dormitories, faculty and residential housing, student services, and facilities for athletics, performing arts, and IT. The emirate is responsible for comprehensive funding of the arrangement. Yet, as distinct from the incredible pace that has characterized the opening of branch campuses in Dubai and even Doha, NYU Abu Dhabi has been given a window of more than two years to coordinate its curriculum and carry out public relations before opening its doors. This lag time is reflective of the nature of the project.

There is simply no precedent for NYU Abu Dhabi. It will be America's first full-fledged liberal arts research university to open abroad, and its eventual enrollment goal of more than 2,000 students is equally ambitious. All courses will be coeducational. Sexton believes NYU is destined to become a "global network university," and the development of operations in Abu Dhabi represents a crucial step toward the eventual establishment of affiliated NYU branches throughout the world's most important metropolitan centers. Sexton contends, "We found in Abu Dhabi a commitment to the notion that the world that is emerging is going to have eight or ten idea capitals in it, driven at their core by research universities, these places where ideas are created…the single thing to understand is that this is not a business investment for Abu Dhabi, this is a deep investment in creating an idea capital" (Krieger, "New York U. plans to open a 'comprehensive liberal-arts campus' in Abu Dhabi," 2007).

NYU has not been recruited to quickly and neatly plug existing gaps in the labor market. According to education administrators in Abu Dhabi, the emirate is perfectly comfortable with the HCT and some of the indigenous private institutions performing that function (Abdullah Al-Khanbashi, personal communication, September 21, 2008). So while preprofessional majors such as engineering and computer science will be on offer at NYU Abu Dhabi, so will history, music, and philosophy. NYU Abu Dhabi embodies a more long-term strategy. Success will be defined in terms of cultivating an appreciation for research and the liberal arts in the process of creating a healthy society and a sustainable economy (Philip Kennedy, personal communication, September 21, 2008).

Early critics of the initiative have concluded that NYU Abu Dhabi's enrollment goals are too lofty. As a means of building local awareness and momentum for its plans, NYU Abu Dhabi established the NYU Abu Dhabi Institute, which hosts locally based conferences, lectures, and cultural activities. Early returns have been somewhat disappointing. Dr. Kennedy, the Institute's director, concedes, "We're trying to build an audience and there are lot of things going on in Abu Dhabi but not this kind of thing…. I don't know if there's a culture of audiences attending lectures…. You don't just want the British Embassy expats to come because then you might as well be doing it in London" (Philip Kennedy, personal communication, September 21, 2008).

Many point to the 2009 closing of George Mason University in Ras al-Khaimeh (GMU-RAK) as a cautionary tale. There, GMU-RAK came nowhere near its modest initial enrollment goal of 200 students. Instead, one year into the project in 2006, the campus enrolled 57 students—27 each in business and engineering and three in biology (Lewin, "US universities rush to set up outposts abroad," 2008). Student recruitment faced two main obstacles: first, George Mason had difficulty identifying regional students willing to relocate to smaller, less developed Ras al-Khaimeh; and second, the pool of local students capable of passing the minimum requisite score of 570 on the TOEFL was limited. Zaid Ansari, then acting vice president of GMU-RAK, explained that most test scores "out there in certain pockets of the region are no place near 570." As a result, nearly half of the 164 undergraduates enrolled in the 2007–08 academic year were taking the remedial English program needed to gain entrance to the university (Mills, "US universities negotiate tricky terrain in the Middle East," 2008).

Abu Dhabi has not set a target for Emirati enrollment at NYU Abu Dhabi, and Sexton believes that nationals will likely become only a tiny percentage of the student population. Doha's Education City—in many ways the regional standard-bearer for successful transnational higher education efforts—provides added context and also stark contrast. Each of the Education City campuses strives to meet specific benchmarks established by Qatar Foundation for the number of enrolled Qataris. A mostly local, multifaceted student recruitment strategy is in use. Since 2001, Education City has played home to the Academic Bridge Program (ABP), a major component of the Qatar Foundation mission. The ABP offers graduating high school students between one and two years of coursework in preparatory English, science, math, computers, and multimedia skills classes. To similar ends, Texas A&M at Qatar (TAMUQ) has developed the Aggie Opportunity Program (AOP). Upon completion of 24 course hours with a minimum grade point average of 2.0, the AOP offers full-time status to provisional students. The foundational scheme enables TAMUQ to effectively increase the number of Qatari students admitted—seven of nine Qataris enrolled in the 2006–2007 academic year were later welcomed as full-time students (Texas A&M University at Qatar, 2008, p. 39). Lastly, considerable outreach has been directed at Qatar and the surrounding Gulf states. Georgetown University School of Foreign Services in Qatar, for example, made more than 30 visits to Qatari high schools during a five-month span in 2007 (Georgetown SFS-Q, 2008). At present, Qatari nationals make up 46 percent of the Education City student population. And, importantly, total enrollment is modest—the classes of 2009 totaled a mere 200 graduates.[4]

Simply put, to approach its more ambitious enrollment goals, NYU Abu Dhabi will have to appeal to expatriates. This is certainly in line with NYU's hopes for an enhanced international profile, but it is a noticeable departure from Abu Dhabi's historically apprehensive stance toward expatriates. Indeed, early critics have questioned the emirate's motivations in developing a university dependent on a global catchment area for its sustainability. The Abu Dhabi Executive Policy Agenda (2007) offers a blunt rejoinder: "In order to keep pace with its rapid economic growth, the Emirate of Abu Dhabi will continue to require large numbers of expatriate workers, particularly as economic diversification drives expansion into labour-intensive sectors such as tourism, real estate and medium and heavy industries" (UAE Executive Council, 2007, p. 35).

Where it pertains to higher education, the policy shift is rather subtler, even consistent with Abu Dhabi's traditional conservatism. Additional tertiary capacity is being supplied by new initiatives, both public and private. For the federal institutions, funding formulas that allocate resources on a per-student basis are presently being put into place. This is meant to address many of the longstanding resource issues that have plagued the public tertiary system while allowing the existing federal institutions to take on more students. Moreover, a new state-of-the-art campus is being designed for UAE University, and Zayed University will be relocated to the new Abu Dhabi Capital District. Together, these policies suggest that Abu Dhabi will try to reverse the longstanding neglect of the federation's public tertiary institutions.

When taken as a whole, however, the system is unmistakably privatizing. Policymakers in Abu Dhabi have been clear on this point: as pressure to provide quality higher education capacity builds, an expanded private sector will be expected to "deliver more educational services on behalf of the government" (Abu Dhabi Executive Council, 2007, p. 28). Yet, in keeping with the emirate's historical concern for demography, Abu Dhabi has only allowed powerful indigenous families to take up the task of establishing its private schools. Prominent examples of this include ALHOSN University (established 2005 with the university slogan, "Global Knowledge with Local Vision") and Abu Dhabi University (established 2003, "Universal Knowledge, Timeless Truth"). Admissions standards for these universities are relatively low, with the end result being that Emiratis are able to enroll locally in large numbers and the federal institutions are relieved of pressure to supply capacity.

It should be remembered that this contrasts markedly with the free-zone strategy currently employed in Dubai. There, universities from more than a dozen countries have been afforded the chance to appeal to students of broad intellectual capability on a largely national basis. Conversely, because of their high admissions standards, NYU Abu Dhabi and the Sorbonne Abu Dhabi will attract only the most intellectually talented students. Together, the two universities will make up Abu Dhabi's elite tertiary sector, a high-profile pairing intended to compliment the emirate's bid to become a cultural hub for the world's pool of luxury tourists. Abu Dhabi has taken some bold steps in the field of higher education, but they are not all in the same direction, and they are not nearly as hurried as those taken in Dubai.

Conclusion: Toward Policy Convergence?

In September 2008, Warren Fox, executive director of higher education for the Dubai KHDA, told *The National*, "We need more branch campuses and we need more variety.... There are areas such as trade, logistics and construction, where large numbers of graduates are needed" (Bardsley, "Economy needs more graduates," 2008). Since then, the global economic downturn has taken an especially heavy toll on Dubai, and the emirate's needs and capabilities have required a major recalibration.

Not long ago, Dubai was generally understood to be a shining example of stability in an otherwise unstable region. Its model for economic diversification and hydro-carbon-independent growth were thought to be worthy of emulation. But the January 2009 announcement of Dubai's $80 billion debt by Nasser al Shaikh, then head of Dubai's finance department, confirmed that the reality was always far more complicated than that. It has set in motion important speculation, not least the actual size of Dubai's debt. Some analysts estimate that it may be as much as $150 billion when accounting for Dubai Holding, the massive government-owned conglomerate. Dubai Holding is the parent company of TECOM Investments, the subsidiary operating Dubai Knowledge Village and Dubai International Academic City.

Additionally, the wisdom of a diversification strategy dependent on property, luxury tourism, and construction—all of which require a consistent infusion of foreign direct investment and steady international credit markets—has come under increased scrutiny. The February 2009 purchase of a five-year, $10 billion bond by the United Arab Emirates central bank has added to uncertainty over Dubai's future: will the recipient of a lifeline from Abu Dhabi be able to retain the autonomy that has defined it for so many years?

To date, Dubai and Abu Dhabi have employed very different higher education strategies, each of which reflects their different views over the desired demographic composition and economic makeup of the UAE. This may change, however, as higher education credentials are increasingly used to ration sparse employment opportunities. The public sector, historically a source of comfortable employment for Emiratis, is thought to be saturated. Recent Emiratization laws intended to protect nationals in the private sector may actually discourage companies from hiring them in significant numbers. Together, these issues could jeopardize the stability of the rentier social and economic system of the UAE. Tensions among Dubai's communities could occur if nationals perceive that the benefits of this system are becoming less obvious.

Perhaps most ominously, a March report issued by EFG-Hermes, an Egyptian investment bank, estimated that Dubai's population stood to decline by 17 percent during 2009 (Bowman, "Dubai population to plummet 17 pct in '09," 2009). Such an exodus would stand to restructure the Dubai job market, further depress local property values, and lead to a decrease in consumer spending.

Given a dwindling expatriate population, the financial viability of Dubai's free-zone universities is hardly assured. If Dubai chooses to build on its free-zone higher education strategy, it will signal a continued reliance on foreign direct investment and perhaps even the de facto training of its remaining non-national communities. In the context of a faltering local economy and a tight job market, this may not be as acceptable as it had been during the economic boom years.

While there has been much speculation about Abu Dhabi's added leverage over neighboring Dubai, the pressure to conform to policies that more consistently advantage Emiratis may not stem from Abu Dhabi, but instead from Dubai's own national population. As a crucial means of rationing scarce employment, higher education strategies that have been divergent in the past could begin to reflect a more uniform preference for the social promotion of Emiratis. An economic downturn and the uncertain benefits of rentierism in tomorrow's Dubai would serve as justification.

---

[1] Zayed University received accreditation from the Middle States Commission on Higher Education—America's accrediting agencies are also increasingly active abroad.

[2] Wyatt Hume, former provost of the University of California system, has been tagged as the new provost of UAEU. Daniel Johnson, former president emeritus of the University of Toledo, was recently appointed provost of Zayed University.

[3] Kuwait spent 7.1 percent in the same year.

[4] For more information on the comparative enrollment strategies of Qatari and Emirati branch campuses, see Witte, 2010.

REFERENCES

Al Karam, A., & Ashencaen, A. (2004). Knowledge village: Establishing a global destination for education in Dubai. Retrieved from http://www.britishcouncil.org/goingglobal-session-2-1225-thursday-tne-abdulla-al-karam-paper.pdf

Bardsley, D. (2008, September 10). University warns of overexpansion. *The National.* Retrieved from http://www.thenational.ae/article/20080910/NATIONAL/886100743&SearchID=73348861050579

Bardsley, D. (2008, September 23). No free zone for universities in capital. *The National.* Retrieved from http://www.thenational.ae/article/20080923/NATIONAL/556313281

Bardsley, D. (2008, September 26). Economy needs more graduates. *The National.* Retrieved from http://www.thenational.ae/article/20080925/NATIONAL/95275055&SearchID=73348861050579

Bardsley, D. (2008, December 7). Tuition fees checked by universities' expansion. *The National.* Retrieved from http://www.thenational.ae/article/20081207/NATIONAL/640032666&SearchID=73348861050579

Bardsley, D. (2010, January 22). University's half-price tuition scheme gets disappointing pass rate. *The National.* Retrieved from http://www.thenational.ae/apps/pbcs.dll/article?AID=/20100122/NATIONAL/701219866/1010

Birks, J. S. (1988). The demographic challenge in the Arab Gulf. In B. R. Pridham (Ed.), *The Arab Gulf and the Arab World.* London: Croom Helm.

Bowman, D. (2009, March 28). Dubai population to plummet 17 pct in '09. *Maktoob Business.* Retrieved from http://business.maktoob.com/20090000000135/Dubai_population_to_plummet_17_pct_in_09/Article.htm

Bristol-Rhys, J. (2008). The dilemma of gender-separated education in the United Arab Emirates. In C. M. Davidson and P. Mackenzie-Smith (Eds.), *Higher education in the Gulf States: Shaping economies, politics and culture.* London: Saqi Books.

Cohen, D. (2005, September 16). Australian university closes campus in United Arab Emirates in dispute with government. *The Chronicle of Higher Education.* Retrieved from http://chronicle.com/weekly/v52/i04/04a04402.htm

Davidson, C. M. (2007). The emirates of Abu Dhabi and Dubai: Contrasting roles in the international system. *Asian Affairs, 38*(1), 33–48.

Davidson, C. M. (2008a). *Dubai: The vulnerability of success.* New York: Columbia University Press.

Davidson, C. M. (2008b). From traditional to formal education in the lower Arabian Gulf, 1820–1971. *History of Education, 37*(5), 633–643.

Davidson, C. M. (2008c). Higher education in the Gulf: A historical background. In C. M. Davidson and P. Mackenzie-Smith (Eds.), *Higher education in the Gulf States: Shaping economies, politics and culture.* London: Saqi Books.

Fattah, H. M., & El Sawy, N. (2005, December 4). Young Iranians follow dreams to Dubai. *The New York Times.* Retrieved from http://www.nytimes.com/2005/12/04/international/middleeast/04dubai.html

Fenelon, K. G. (1973). The United Arab Emirates: An economic and social survey. London: Longman.

Fox, W. (2008). The United Arab Emirates and policy priorities for higher education. In C. M. Davidson and P. Mackenzie-Smith (Eds.), *Higher education in the Gulf States: Shaping economies, politics and culture.* London: Saqi Books.

Georgetown University School of Foreign Service in Qatar. (2008). Annual report 2007–2008.

Halloran, W. F. (1999). Zayed University: A new model for higher education in the United Arab Emirates. In *Education and the Arab World: Challenges of the next millennium*. London: I.B. Tauris.

Heard-Bey, F. (1982). From trucial states to United Arab Emirates. London: Longman.

Janardhan, N. (2006). Managing foreign workforce in the Gulf: Redefining the rules of engagement. [Conference proceedings]. *8th Asian Security Conference*, New Delhi, India.

Krieger, Z. (2007, October 19). Dubai aiming to be an academic hub, strikes a deal with Michigan State. *The Chronicle of Higher Education*. Retrieved from http://chronicle.com/weekly/v54/i08/08a03301.htm

Krieger, Z. (2007, October 26). New York U. plans to open a 'comprehensive liberal-arts campus' in Abu Dhabi. *The Chronicle of Higher Education*. Retrieved from http://chronicle.com/weekly/v54/i09/09a04501.htm

Krieger, Z. (2008, March 28). An academic building boom transforms the Persian Gulf. *The Chronicle of Higher Education*. Retrieved from http://chronicle.com/weekly/v54/i29/29a02601.htm

Lewin, T. (2008, February 10). US universities rush to set up outposts abroad. *The New York Times*. Retrieved from http://www.nytimes.com/2008/02/10/education/10global.html

McMurtrie, B. (2006, November 10). Overseas programs increasingly sharing risk with host countries. *The Chronicle of Higher Education*. Retrieved from http://chronicle.com/weekly/v53/i12/12a04202.htm

Mills, A. (2008, July 25). US universities negotiate tricky terrain in the Middle East. *The Chronicle of Higher Education*. Retrieved from http://chronicle.com/article/US-Universities-Negotiate/19462

Mills, A. (2008, September 26). Emirates look to the West for prestige. *The Chronicle of Higher Education*. Retrieved from http://chronicle.com/weekly/v55/i05/05a00101.htm

Nicks-McCaleb, L. (2005). The impact of state funded higher education on neighborhood and community in the United Arab Emirates. *International Education Journal, 6*(3), 322–33.

Peck, M. (1986). The United Arab Emirates: A venture in unity. London: Croom Helm.

Sakr, N. (1980). Federalism in the United Arab Emirates: Prospects and regional implications. In T. Niblock (Ed.), *Social and economic development in the Arab Gulf*. London: Croom Helm.

Shihab, M. (2001). Economic development in the UAE. In I. Abed and P. Hellyer (Eds.), *United Arab Emirates: A new perspective*. London: Trident Press.

Texas A&M University at Qatar. (2008). Annual report 2007–2008.

UAE Executive Council. (2007). *Policy agenda 2007–2008: The emirate of Abu Dhabi*. Retrieved from http://gsec.abudhabi.ae/Sites/GSEC/Navigation/EN/publications,did=90344.html

UAE MOHESR. (2007). *Educating the next generation of Emiratis: A master plan for UAE higher education*. Retrieved from http://planipolis.iiep.unesco.org/upload/United%20Arab%20Emirates/United%20Arab%20Emirates_Higher_Education_plan.pdf

UAE National Media Council. (2009). *UAE at a glance 2009*. Retrieved from http://www.uaeinteract.com/government/

Urban Planning Council. (2007). *Plan Abu Dhabi 2030*. Retrieved from http://www.abudhabi.ae/egovPoolPortal_WAR/appmanager/ADeGP/Citizen?_nfpb=true&_pageLabel=P40001297212175920 68983&lang=en

Walters, T. N., Kadragic, A., & Walters, L. M. (2006). Miracle or mirage: Is development sustainable in the United Arab Emirates? *The Middle East Review of International Affairs, 10*(3), 4.

Witte, S. (2010). Gulf State branch campuses: Global student recruitment. *International Higher Education, 58*. Retrieved from http://www.bc.edu/bc_org/avp/soe/cihe/newsletter/Number58/p5_Witte.htm

World Bank. (2008). *The road not traveled: Education reform in the Middle East and North Africa*. Retrieved from http://siteresources.worldbank.org/INTMENA/Resources/EDU_Flagship_Full_ENG.pdf

Chapter Three

HIGHER EDUCATION CREATES HIGHER EXPECTATIONS IN JORDAN: COMBATING THE LOSS OF THE KINGDOM'S INTELLECTUAL WEALTH

ROBERT G. AYAN JR., MANAGING PARTNER, CAMBRIDGE ADVISORS LLC

One way that higher education creates value in societies is by preparing students for employment and entrepreneurship. However, higher education itself is insufficient to create these opportunities; the wider political and social context must also be favorable. A country like Jordan may continue to make gains in higher education, but still face related challenges that cannot be ignored, such as creating jobs for the many unemployed. With a population of approximately six million and a "youth bulge"— 53 percent of the population is under the age of 25 according to 2008 estimates— Jordan faces major socioeconomic challenges today, with even greater challenges ahead. In recognition of these trends, Jordan has begun new educational initiatives that aim, in part, to match the rising expectations of graduates with employment opportunities that suit their skills and aspirations. This article will explore one such initiative, the El Hassan Science City, in particular detail.

Official estimates place unemployment in Jordan at 13 percent for 2008, with unofficial estimates reaching as high as 30 percent. The poverty rate is estimated at 14.2 percent. Persons under 30 years of age represent 75 percent of total unemployment, making youth unemployment a major concern. High unemployment is accompanied by low labor force participation rates—12.6 percent for females and 66.7 percent for males (Kabbani & Kothari, 2005). Gender differences are apparent in both unemployment and labor force participation statistics, which suggest a situation that is unfavorable to women.

Labor force participation rates, however, have been increasing appreciably for females over the past four decades, with a sixfold increase since 1961, when 1.9 percent of women participated in the labor force. This is, in part, the result of an increase in educational attainment among women. Meanwhile, higher fertility rates and enrollment ratios among the youth mean a greater number of dependents, and combined with greater male emigration, the picture starts to become clearer: Jordan has been progressing positively in education enrollment and labor force participation against its own historical benchmarks. Jordanians are increasingly expecting education to yield greater benefits in terms of employment, which makes the challenges of the unemployment situation all the more urgent (Al-Khaldi, 2006).

FIGURE 3.1: THE YOUTH BULGE—JORDAN'S POPULATION PYRAMID FOR 2010

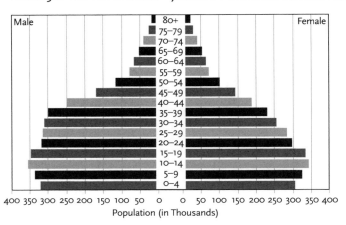

In spite of much progress, Jordan still needs to create 200,000 new jobs by the year 2015 to keep up with the more than 35,000 new job seekers that enter the labor market each year. In addition, about 175,000 jobs are needed to address current unemployment figures. Jordan has generated about 55,000 jobs per year on average from 1995–2006, but more than 50 percent of those jobs have gone to non-Jordanians. The large youth bulge approaching the labor market beyond the next six years will further exacerbate unemployment. Investments in education have succeeded in raising the level of education of each generation, but expectations for better jobs and higher wages have also increased, meaning that the simple number of jobs created is less important than their type and quality (Assaad & Amer, 2007).

Studies on the education level attained by the labor force in Jordan have shown that unemployment stands at 11 percent among those with a secondary education, while the corresponding figure for those with more than a secondary education is 28 percent (Kabbani & Kothari, 2005; World Bank, 2008). A longitudinal study of these groups shows that, by 1999, 19.4 percent of the Jordanian labor force held a university degree, a figure that has increased substantially since Jordan began making its first investments in higher education with the establishment of Jordan University in 1962. Again, a relative comparison shows that Jordan is making positive progress against historical benchmarks, while international benchmarks reveal that much room for improvement remains. Rising expectations are therefore a positive by-product of successful investments in education in Jordan, but they mean that Jordan must keep pace by adapting to the new social and economic dynamics of a more educated society.

Education, Employment, and Entrepreneurship are Paths to Emigration

Across the Arab world, an average of 26 percent of young people say that they would permanently migrate to another country if given the opportunity, and this desire is expressed by roughly one-third of young men. Alarmingly, it turns out that "a country's greatest assets are also its most mobile": those most likely to express a desire to move abroad include those with at least four years of postsecondary education (26 percent), full-time employees (31 percent), and people planning to start a business (36 percent) (Silatech, 2010). It appears there is a clear correlation between individual ambition and a desire to move abroad: the greater the ambition, the greater the desire to move abroad to seek better opportunities. With nearly one million Jordanians living outside the country, most would recognize that these conditions prevail in Jordan.

The Jordanian economy exhibits the major characteristics of a "rentier" economy, with substantial public revenues derived from exported natural resources and external aid. Four characteristics determine whether a state may be described as "rentier":

- If rent situations predominate;
- If the economy relies on a substantial external rent—and therefore does not require a strong domestic productive sector;
- If only a small proportion of the working population is actually involved in the generation of the rent;
- And, perhaps most importantly, if the state's government is the principal recipient of the external rent. (Beblawi, 1990)

In this classic definition of a rentier economy, a minority of the population is involved in the generation of rent while the majority of the population is engaged in its distribution and consumption. Jordan differs from the classic definition in that much of household income is also a product of remittances from abroad, in which the state does not act as a direct intermediary. However, the real danger of rentierism is in the mentality that it creates and its effect on the expectations, work ethic, and productivity of members of society. The rentier mentality is defined as a

> ...psychological condition with profound consequences for productivity: contracts are given as an expression of gratitude rather than as a reflection of economic rationale; civil servants see their principal duty as being available in their offices during working hours; businessmen abandon industry and enter into real-estate speculation or other special situations associated with a booming oil sector; the best and brightest abandon business and seek out lucrative government employment; manual labor and other work considered demeaning by the rentier is farmed out to foreign workers, whose remittances flood out of the rentier economy; and so on. In extreme cases income is derived simply from citizenship. (Yates, 1996, p. 22)

Ideally, societies should employ a holistic, systemic approach to achieving long-term socioeconomic development through sound public policy that complements the value creation of education with the value capture of employment and entrepreneurship. In contrast, the immediacy of existing socioeconomic pressures can lead to thinking that focuses resources on the short term and relies on direct methods that are not necessarily aligned with higher-value objectives.

With unemployment, poverty, and the rising youth bulge as drivers, Jordan has sought to create jobs wherever it can. This often leads to mass employment schemes designed to employ the largest segments of Jordanian society, which result in a "race to the bottom" in which workers compete for low-wage, low-skilled jobs—a race that Jordan will lose, regardless of the number of short-term winners. This strategy has been further exacerbated by an assortment of macro- and microeconomic policies that encourage educated Jordanians to move abroad with the short-term expectation that they will remit a significant portion of their income to family members back home.

This "race to the bottom" has already attracted foreign guest workers to Jordan in large numbers, competing for low-wage, low-skilled jobs that are largely intended for underprivileged and less educated Jordanians. Although the government creates tax incentives to support this kind of employment, businesses that benefit from the incentives are free to source from a global labor pool. This has resulted in many Egyptians, Bangladeshis, Malaysians, Indonesians, Chinese, Burmese, and others working in Jordan in industries ranging from textiles to construction. Current estimates are that the number of foreign guest workers exceeds the number of unemployed Jordanians, with 250,000–300,000 foreign guest workers and 175,000 unemployed Jordanians. More importantly, the Jordanian government also reports that 52–63 percent of newly created jobs were filled by foreign guest workers (World Bank, 2008). In a study on the paradox of concurrent economic growth and high unemployment in Jordan published by the World Bank (2008),

...three crucial mismatches explain the simultaneous existence of increasing labor demand:

- *Geography*: New jobs and prospective workers are far apart.
- *Employability*: Although Jordanian workers have sufficient education, vocational training, and job experience, employers often prefer foreign workers because of their workplace behavior and productivity.
- *Expectations*: Jordanians maintain a false optimism about their employment prospects and earning potential.

Perhaps these conclusions give further credence to the notion that Jordanians indeed have higher expectations, whether resulting from dissatisfaction with available job opportunities and wages, the inflated expectations generated by rentierism, or other cultural factors.

Jordan employs a large segment of its population today through the public sector—more than one-third of the workforce of 1.5 million—which itself has influenced the development in the culture of a "social security" mentality, in which guarantees of public-sector employment have tremendous appeal. With over two-thirds of the population under the age of 30, it is clear that this fast-approaching youth bulge, combined with high public-sector employment, high unemployment, the influx of foreign guest workers, competitively disadvantaged industries, and increasing competition from abroad, will cause Jordan's economy to face a crisis in the not-too-distant future. If left unaddressed, these dynamics could exacerbate unemployment and perhaps lead to social unrest.

The demographic pressures represented by the youth bulge, the high birth rate, and the continued loss of Jordan's intellectual wealth to competing economies create an unsustainable future where Jordan invests in education without capturing the value it creates. Continued investment in education makes Jordan a donor to competing economies in the form of tens of billions of dollars in human capital, including the loss of Jordanian faculty—an attack at the start of Jordan's socioeconomic value chain. In addition, rising living standards, exposure to ever-greater amenities and luxuries, and even images broadcast into homes from satellite television create a broader set of rising expectations across Jordanian society for an ever-increasing quality of life that Jordan can never support through low-wage, low-skilled employment.

FIGURE 3.2: JORDANIAN SOCIETY WITH YOUTH BULGE AND LOSS OF TALENT

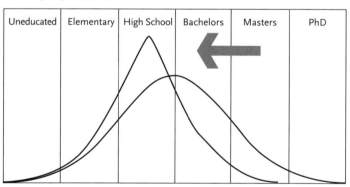

Illustrative graph of Jordanian society with combined impact of youth bulge and loss of educated talent leading to the regression of society (the "race to the bottom").

If Jordan fails to create sufficient opportunity through employment or entrepreneurship to enable the most educated members of society to meet their rising expectations, they will continue to leave the country in greater numbers, diminishing the capacity of the local workforce and regressing Jordanian society as measured by education levels (figure 3.2). Combined with the youth bulge and the poverty cycle generated by a historical emphasis on creating low-wage, low-skilled employment opportunities, Jordanians may find less incentive to pursue higher education, except as motivated by their values or as a means to emigrate. Indeed, higher education is often viewed as a path to emigration, and "brain waste" typically precedes "brain drain." The desired result of socioeconomic development is lost, as are other benefits associated with an educated populace, such as progress in the arts, sciences, culture, democracy, and human rights.

FIGURE 3.3: JORDANIAN SOCIETY BY EDUCATION LEVEL ATTAINMENT, 1999–2008

	Uneducated	Elementary	High School	Intermediate Diploma	Bachelors	Higher Diploma	Masters	Ph.D
1999	519,832	1,400,909	456,629	227,536	194,800	6,527	18,386	7,280
2008	387,661	1,651,159	644,810	285,101	381,409	7,822	32,186	11,967
	Education Level							

Source: National Center for Human Resource Development, Amman, Jordan

Over the past decade, it is clear that more Jordanians have been pursuing higher education (figure 3.3), even if Jordan continues to lose many members of its educated class. As a country that values education, how can Jordan compete across the set of drivers that can stem the continued loss of its human capital and allow it to capture the value it creates from investments in education? Furthermore, where and how can high-value jobs that will leverage Jordan's investment in higher education be created? If higher education creates higher expectations, and higher expectations consequently lead to higher rates of emigration in search of opportunity, then clearly greater emphasis needs to be placed on identifying ways to retain the intellectual wealth of the country both by investing in and making use of their talents.

Applying Best Practices to Higher Education Management

Societies worldwide share a common desire to advance themselves through higher education, yet continued investments in higher education alone are not always realized in socioeconomic returns. Many developing societies lose their most talented people immediately after they graduate, and as in Jordan, education is one path to emigration. The lack of suitable advanced degree programs is another cause for the ambitious to find their way to societies that can offer them higher levels of education and more attractive opportunities in their preferred field of study after graduation. Meanwhile, the climate for entrepreneurship in many places stifles the ability of entrepreneurs to develop businesses locally, making emigration all the more attractive. In a country like Jordan, the naturally small market will force many entrepreneurs to look abroad to more attractive markets.

There is arguably never enough money for higher education and research, and indeed, as fundamental drivers of socioeconomic development, governments and organizations in the Arab region need to invest more in human capacity-building to continue to advance Arab societies. Of the 385 universities across the entire Arab world, not one has been consistently ranked among the top 500 universities world-wide, let alone among the top 100. In addition, Arab universities on average spend only 1 percent of their budgets on research, while the international average for research universities is 35 percent.

With Jordan already spending 6.5 percent of GDP on education, as compared to 5.3 percent in the Arab region, and with 20 percent of Jordan's state budget directed toward education, it may appear that Jordan is doing all that it can to fund education. While developed countries spend 8 percent of GDP on education and their GDP is much larger, Jordan's youth bulge creates higher demands for expenditures on educa-tion. Therefore, even 8 percent of GDP might be grossly insufficient given the demo-graphics of Jordanian society and the size of Jordan's GDP.

Today, it is difficult to justify allocating more than 20 percent of the state budget to education when society has so many pressing needs. However, as an optimization problem, the government will have to determine priorities, eliminate sources of waste, increase responsibly the role of the private sector, and set the proper expectation on the cost of quality education in Jordan to have all members of society meet their responsibilities. Further, more capital-efficient approaches to higher education and research can come from involving academic institutions in the research activities of the Kingdom. Investments in higher education, complemented by greater innovation and entrepreneurship, should allow the government to realize greater tax revenues. Only greater value-capture from higher education and research can effectively allow the government to continuously reinvest in education.

The Arab world rarely sees a society come together to create an indigenous, non-government (private), not-for-profit institute of higher education or scientific research that represents an investment in its collective future. It is equally rare to find Arab academic and research institutions in possession of significant endowments that are invested for financial returns in order to increase the annual budgets available for higher education and research. The oldest modern example in the region is perhaps the American University of Beirut (AUB), originally founded in 1866 by Protestant missionaries as the Syrian Protestant College, which possessed a $637 million endow-ment in 2008. The newest example is likely the King Abdullah University for Science and Technology (KAUST) in the Kingdom of Saudi Arabia, which in 2010 was esti-mated to have a $10 billion endowment. In Jordan, two state universities, Jordan University and Yarmouk University, have modest investment funds and have benefited over the last few years from returns accrued to these funds (Khasawneh, Bataineh,

Nazer, Qudais, & Al-Akhal, 2008, p. 51). The vast majority of universities in the Arab world are of two personalities: the overcrowded, underfunded state school that relies on taxes and tuition, or the private, for-profit universities that often utilize attractive American branding, where quality and accreditation varies widely, and higher education is exploited as a cash-cow, dividend-paying business.

It is noble to keep the high cost of education at a minimum for students, and the principle of "*education maximization* versus *revenue maximization*" (figure 3.4) is exactly why it is all the more important for institutions of higher education and scientific research to develop business models that: 1) increase the financial sustainability of the institution by generating wealth from multiple income streams, and 2) simultaneously develop programs that maintain the highest standards of quality. *Revenue maximization* supports both *profit maximization* and *education maximization*. Thus, for not-for-profit institutions whose principal intention is to serve society, *education maximization* and *revenue maximization* are complementary concepts rather than opposing forces. In contrast, with for-profit institutions, *revenue maximization* supports *profit maximization*. Inversely, *education maximization* means maximizing education even if that means charging higher tuition or fees. Therefore, in economic terms, *education maximization* is an optimization problem in which institutions decide how best to balance academic relevance and quality with affordability, capital efficiency, and return on investment.

FIGURE 3.4: EDUCATION MAXIMIZATION VERSUS REVENUE MAXIMIZATION IN HIGHER EDUCATION

Education Maximization		
High	Capital efficient, characteristic of a quality non-profit teaching university trying to keep tuition low.	Quality is expensive, typical of a research university receiving supplementary sources of revenue or with an endowment.
Low	Capital inefficient, characteristic of an overcrowded, underfunded state school forced to optimize on quantity over quality and trying to minimize costs at the expense of quality.	Characteristic of a for-profit, private university seeking to profit from the need for higher education where quality and accreditation are often lacking.
	Low	High

Revenue Maximization

The fundamentals of profit maximization: If Jordanian universities can diversify their sources of income, they can achieve revenue maximization to support education maximization before increasing class sizes, raising tuition, or trying to keep costs artificially low.

With its 27 universities, Jordan has the ability to demonstrate how education and research can be accomplished, even for the resource-poor, by adopting a model that is sustainable and exhibits maximum capital efficiency. Such a model will be built around a well-conceived business plan that provides multiple income streams to support higher education and research based upon global best practices. Adopting and adapting these global best practices for the Jordanian context is one of the primary tasks of El Hassan Science City, a new Jordanian initiative that is discussed below. It is highly anticipated that the Science City will serve as a model that can be replicated at other institutions across Jordan and the region.

A Race to the Top: Building a Knowledge-Based Economy

Globalization allows corporations to create greater competition in their supply chain, which drives down prices and makes consumers better off by passing on lower costs of production in the form of lower-priced goods. Thus, technology, productivity, and value creation are major competitive dimensions of globalization that counter the "race to the bottom" dynamic that globalization generates in search of greater capital efficiency. At the same time, the mobility of industry is a tremendous threat to job security, since companies that are constantly in search of lower costs of production and lower wages can abandon one country in favor of another. With local industry in Jordan often more interested in imitation rather than innovation, lower trade barriers leave these businesses vulnerable to more efficient and more dynamic competitors from abroad. This competition creates incentives for countries desperate for job creation to relax regulations on the environment and workers' rights, and to pursue other policies that have adverse impacts on human security. In addition, rapid global industrialization and the rising living standards associated with greater consumer choice have led to unprecedented rises in commodity prices for food, energy, and other critical inputs. This has jeopardized the health, safety, and well-being of vulnerable communities worldwide.

Jordanian industry cannot compete globally on cost of labor and inputs in this context, so it must compete by increasing demand for its goods and services while commanding higher prices to offset higher costs. These dynamics logically lead to one conclusion: in order to command premium prices, Jordan must create value in the form of premium products and services, not basic commodities or labor. This naturally places Jordan in a "race to the top," yet most mass employment schemes today engage Jordan in competition for the lowest-wage, lowest-skilled jobs, reflecting an acceptance of a lower standard of living for Jordanians that contradicts their rising expectations.

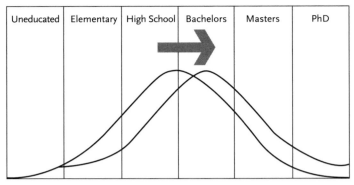

| Uneducated | Elementary | High School | Bachelors | Masters | PhD |

Illustrative graph of Jordanian society advancing as a whole. The arrow shows the impact of creating high-value employment, utilizing the highly educated members of society to employ all other segments—the "race to the top."

By focusing on Jordan's best and brightest, those who can generate wealth and employment opportunities for all other segments of society, directly or indirectly, policy makers can help Jordanian society advance as a whole. The alternative is to witness the continued bifurcation of society into separate economies, cultures, and communities with deepening divides of education, occupation, and geographic location (Florida, 2002). While other mass employment schemes focus on the low-skilled, low-wage earning segments, the new El Hassan Science City initiative differentiates itself by focusing on Jordan's intellectual wealth—the most educated and entrepreneurial members of society—to create high-growth industries and high-value employment, engaging Jordan in a "race to the top."

Science Cities as Engines for Economic Growth

Across the Arab world, new initiatives are demonstrating the increasing value placed on education and the link between education and employment. One of the best-publicized examples is Qatar's Education City, which represents a multibillion-dollar investment by the Qatar Foundation to create branch campuses, predominantly of American universities, in Qatar. Qatar's Education City contains the Qatar Science and Technology Park (QSTP), an initiative designed to foster a climate conducive to R&D and technology commercialization. The $330 million facilities of QSTP were donated by the Qatar Foundation, but are expected to be financially independent in the future. The ambition of this project exceeds the relative size of Qatar's population of about 1.2 million, yet aims to position Qatar in the longer term as a regional hub for education, science, and technology with the help of world-class institutions from the United States and the financial backing of the Qatar Foundation. The set of drivers and the context fueling the Qatari initiative differs greatly from that of Jordan, which requires a solution that fits its own unique set of challenges and circumstances.

Jordan is taking its own approach through a new initiative, named El Hassan Science City in honor of the highly decorated statesman and humanitarian HRH Prince El Hassan bin Talal from whom it takes its inspiration. El Hassan Science City is an integrated science park that combines the value creation of education and research institutions with the value capture of entrepreneurship and employment. This systematic approach is a means of continuing the advancement of Jordanian society as a whole from a largely underdeveloped country at the time of independence to a country known for its human capital and leading academic institutions. The Science City was inaugurated on April 17, 2007 by His Majesty King Abdullah II, and is currently being developed under the leadership of HRH Princess Sumaya bint El Hassan, who as President of the Royal Scientific Society and Chairman of the Princess Sumaya University of Technology, two leading academic and research institutions on the campus, is actively leading the effort.

Science parks generally offer an ideal habitat for knowledge-based enterprises and institutions. They promote the economic development and competitiveness of countries, regions, cities, and economic sectors by:

- Enhancing the synergy between government, industry, and academia;
- Creating new business opportunities and adding value to mature companies and industries;
- Fostering entrepreneurship and incubating new innovative enterprises;
- Building productive environments for enterprising knowledge workers; and
- Generating high-value, knowledge-based employment.

As an integrated science park, the Science City will offer increasing returns to scale and economies of scale through the synergies and efficiencies of clustered academic, research, industrial, and entrepreneurial activities on its campus (O'Flaherty, 2005). Thus, it aims to create and capture value with maximum capital efficiency and with the goal of increasingly generating wealth that will be reinvested in higher education and research. The Science City's leadership understands that investing in knowledge pays the highest returns, especially given that productive, committed, creative, and talented people offer unlimited wealth creation potential. As an example, Hsinchu Science and Industrial Park in Taiwan has been successful in developing Taiwan's high-technology economy. It has been particularly helpful in connecting the highly educated and successful Taiwanese expatriate community in Silicon Valley with Taiwan's industrial sector (Saxenian and Hsu, 2001), a dynamic that El Hassan Science City seeks to emulate with its own diaspora.

As a general rule, the output of any organization or society cannot surpass the capabilities of its human capital. Although quality higher education and research programs are expensive to deliver and maintain, any vision for a society or organization starts with the capabilities of its available human capital. In knowledge-based industries in particular, investing in human capital is the only long-term source of sustainable competitive advantage. No society can build a knowledge-based economy without becoming proficient at developing the knowledge worker and building knowledge-based enterprises. Exporting talent is in conflict with these aims, despite the short-term benefits of remittance income.

By focusing on the "job makers" rather than "job seekers," El Hassan Science City has developed a series of resources to incubate Jordan's next economy and create high-value job opportunities directly and indirectly, over time, by focusing on value-capture mechanisms aligned with academic programs and the needs of industry. To succeed, the Science City seeks international partnerships across academic, scientific, and industrial interests to form global communities of action to address the "human imperative," a view espoused by the Science City's leadership, which seeks to place science in the service of humanity and utilize it for peace.

The Science City is establishing research clusters in energy, water, the environment, health technologies, materials, and information and communication technologies to address the common set of challenges that people in the developing and developed worlds face. A new graduate school offering advanced degree programs in science and technology and a recently launched business school will complement the clusters to complete the talent pyramid required for successful new product and venture development. The Science City also includes technology incubators, an entrepreneurship center, and a venture capital fund in development, all of which provide the value capture mechanisms to commercialize innovations. To succeed in developing and maintaining strong academic and research programs, the Science City places a heavy emphasis on international education and global collaborations. Without access to cumulative research and without a solid grasp of markets, customers, and competitors, Jordanians will have a difficult time collaborating, or competing, globally. Global partnerships starting with international education are fundamental to the long-term success of El Hassan Science City.

Another major goal of El Hassan Science City is to replace the phenomenon of "brain drain" with a more multidirectional flow of talent, or "brain circulation," which would allow the Kingdom to gain greater access to leading thinkers. In that sense, El Hassan Science City will convert the ongoing loss of Jordan's human capital into a strategic redistribution of talent to leading economies and centers of innovation worldwide, engaging the Jordanian diaspora community in the activities of El Hassan Science City for the benefit of all. This global diaspora will form a bridge to more technologically advanced societies and centers of innovation, much like other diaspora communities have done for their native countries. It is worth mentioning that more than 59 percent of advanced degrees in science and engineering in the United States are earned by non-Americans, with Chinese, Indian, and Middle Eastern scholars representing the three largest groups in that order (National Science Foundation, 2009). The Princess Sumaya University for Technology, located on the El Hassan Science City campus, continues to host international faculty, and aims to continue to build on the positive experiences it has had in utilizing international institution-to-institution, faculty-to-faculty, and student-to-student relationships to develop world-class educational programs and graduates while maintaining its top spot in national rankings.

The creation of an innovation ecosystem on the campus of El Hassan Science City, and by extension the formation of a national innovation system driven by concerted public policy to develop the intellectual infrastructure of the Kingdom, provides the organization of the human, financial, and material resources needed to effectively build a knowledge-based economy. This organization relies on both top-down and bottom-up methodologies to achieve meaningful, sustainable results on a national level. The largest gains can be made through sound public policy and public administration to catalyze the dynamics of a national innovation system. Achieving successful results at El Hassan Science City through this approach will reinforce decision-making in the government to support a systematic approach to building a knowledge-based economy.

Enterprise Formation and Knowledge as a Competitive Advantage

The resulting formation of knowledge-based industries allows international firms to enter Jordan through acquisition of talent and technology. In 2009, tech giant Yahoo! became the first international company to acquire a Jordanian technology firm, Maktoob.com. This differs from strategies that companies use to expand into larger economies, which focus on acquiring commodity skills sets or access to large consumer markets. In the Jordanian approach, which has already begun to rouse a positive response from the government, talent is the key driver. This provides Jordan with a dominant strategy, since even talented Jordanians who go abroad for a period of time will have higher incomes and greater remittance income potential.

A Jordanian model will emerge that is unique to the context, circumstances, and cultural aspects of the Kingdom. This will necessarily include the full utilization of the trade agreements that the Kingdom has in place with leading economies like the United States to allow for industry to benefit from the economies of scale and scope that larger markets offer. The impact on labor-market demand should reinforce investments in higher education and provide an economic incentive for Jordanians to pursue higher education.

The creation of products, services, and solutions that use Jordanian talent and resources will lead to greater national self-reliance, which will not only help safeguard the Kingdom's independence, but also will increase Jordan's standing as a place where innovative ideas are born. Rising living standards stemming from greater socioeconomic development through the productive capacities of Jordan's intellectual wealth will also advance more of society together, averting its continued bifurcation, and meet the rising expectations that have been driving Jordanians abroad.

Given that entrepreneurship represents the most organic expression of a society's capabilities, further investments in higher education will serve to raise Jordan's capacity and capability for successful new enterprise creation. Value must first be created before being captured: following the success of entrepreneurs, initial investments in

Jordanian enterprises by local, pioneering investors will give rise to foreign, professional investors who will follow the source of innovation back to Jordan. The increased investments will further help retain the intellectual wealth of the country, and support the vision of His Majesty King Abdullah II to create high-value, export-oriented, knowledge-based industries.

With the Science City's approach, the physical colocation and proximity of activities creates an "innovation avenue" that manifests the value chain geographically and physically. Ideas can move from laboratory, schoolroom, and educational facility through the facilitation, networking, and cross-fertilization units of the Science City to commercialization. With such a dynamic, the cycle of value creation terminates with value capture, and then the system recycles. This has been exemplified already by a number of companies that have emerged from El Hassan Science City, such as Ketab (www.ketabtech.com), which develops human–computer interaction technologies. Started by university graduates who were identified through an entrepreneurship competition, Ketab received mentorship at the local technology incubator, where it developed its patented technology and later received early-stage venture capital financing through local angel investors and venture capitalists. Founded in 2007, Ketab now employs over 25 full-time employees and has surpassed breakeven financials. The founders are now active members of the El Hassan Science City entrepreneurship community, and where they mentor successive generations of entrepreneurs.

In today's globalizing economy, national and regional advantage is shifting from comparative advantage based on endowed resources to competitive advantage contingent upon the creation of knowledge-intensive capabilities and clusters that are sustainable, immobile, and inimitable. Often, the competitive advantage is supported by a collaborative advantage that stretches across traditional boundaries, geographies, and disciplines to produce greater novelty. Factories and physical assets can be readily relocated in pursuit of lower costs of input or greater integration within the global supply chain, whereas centers of knowledge and learning cannot. While physical products and low-level services become increasingly commoditized, cutting-edge knowledge increasingly becomes a differentiator. These dynamics can be seen as both an opportunity and a threat, and those who are ready to embrace them as an opportunity will be the ones to reap the greatest benefits.

Further, the speed of competition has also quickened, and national and regional fortunes can change at unprecedented speed. Advantage, once lost, may be extremely difficult to regain. Those who fall behind this curve will find the catch-up extremely tough. Inversely, nations can now go from "developing" to "developed" within the same generation. Technological leapfrogging can advance nations and regions beyond their more advanced neighbors and competitors. Yet the speed and intensity of the competition has also increased, and there is at once both disaggregation and greater mobility, combined with concentration around hubs of knowledge and expertise. Jordan needs to create just such a nexus through this initiative in order to jump ahead and stay ahead.

Conclusion

El Hassan Science City will help Jordan to further diversify its economy by creating knowledge-based enterprises and high-value employment that can outperform other sectors in terms of wealth creation, growth, job creation, exports, and investment. Engaging in a race to the top is a more inflation-resistant strategy that combines the principles of differentiation, value creation, and greater national self-reliance as a means of reducing Jordan's sensitivity to fluctuating global economic pressures. Jordan needs to undergo a comprehensive legal and tax policy review to optimize the country to serve as a platform for innovation and new enterprise creation. Issues to consider include changes in foreign work visas, immigration policies, and bankruptcy laws. The following are other examples of areas of legislation that should be reviewed nationally for their impact on efficient and effective new enterprise creation and growth:

- Intellectual property rights (IPR) and enforcement;
- Tax legislation and tax incentives (including exemptions and credits);
- Bankruptcy legislation;
- Laws on hiring and firing;
- Venture capital fund formation and management;
- Anti-fraud legislation;
- Immigration, visas, and citizenship;
- Incorporation processes and requirements;
- Corporate laws restricting majority ownership of enterprises to members of certain professions and professional associations; and
- Professional licenses.

El Hassan Science City thus aims to incubate Jordan's knowledge-based economy through a holistic, systemic, and systematic approach that constitutes a national strategy to utilize the resources of the Kingdom to address its unique circumstances within the context of its own social and economic development. Institutions and government bodies throughout Jordan are responsible for collecting empirical data and providing analysis of this raw data. The data and analyses provided by these organizations should be the foundation for decision-making, which will allow Jordan to develop a sound participatory, composite national agenda on the basis of collective intelligence.

It is clear that higher education and higher levels of education are raising expectations in Jordan. Jordan now needs to capitalize on its investments by taking a new approach to socioeconomic development that matches the higher expectations of its more educated population. As a pioneering national nonprofit initiative, El Hassan Science City hopes to set an example for the transformation of Jordanian institutions of higher education and the Kingdom's intellectual wealth into powerful engines of social and economic development, with all of Jordanian society as beneficiaries.

REFERENCES

Al-Khaldi, M. D. (2006). Educational attainment of Jordan's population and labor force. *Journal of Social Sciences, 2*(1), 1–6.

Assaad, R., & Amer, M. (2007). *Labor market conditions in Jordan, 1995–2006: An analysis of microdata sources, volume I.* Amman, Jordan: Al-Manar Project, National Center for Human Resource Development.

Beblawi, H. (1990). The rentier state in the Arab world. In Luciani, G. (Ed.), *The Arab state.* London: Routledge.

Florida, R. (2002). *The rise of the creative class: And how it's transforming work, leisure, community, and everyday life.* New York, NY: Basic Books.

Kabbani, N., & Kothari, E. (2005). *Youth employment in the MENA region: A situational assessment.* Washington, DC: World Bank.

Khasawneh, F. E., Bataineh, S. M., Nazer, M. Z., Qudais, M. K. A., & Al-Akhal, R. K. (2008). *Higher education at a glance in Jordan.* Amman, Jordan: National Center for Human Resources Development.

National Science Foundation. (2009, December). *Doctorate recipients from U.S. universities, summary report 2007–2008.*

O'Flaherty, B. (2005). *City economics.* Cambridge, MA: Harvard University Press.

Saxenian, A., & Hsu, J. (2001). Transnational communities and industrial upgrading: The Silicon Valley-Hsinchu connection. *Industrial and Corporate Change, 10*(4), 893–920.

Silatech. (2010, January). *The Silatech index: Voices of young Arabs.* Doha, Qatar: Silatech.

Yates, D. A. (1996). *The rentier state in Africa.* Trenton, NJ: Africa World Press.

World Bank. (2008, December 23). *Hashemite Kingdom of Jordan: Resolving Jordan's labor market paradox of concurrent high economic growth and unemployment.* Washington, DC: World Bank Social and Economic Development Group, Middle East and North Africa Region.

Chapter Four

Strategic Planning in Higher Education in the Middle East: The Case of Non-Gulf Countries

Hana A. El-Ghali, Managing Director, Institute for International
    Studies in Education, University of Pittsburgh
Qianyi Chen, Center Associate, Institute for Higher Education Management,
    University of Pittsburgh
John L. Yeager, Director, Institute for Higher Education Management,
    University of Pittsburgh

For several thousand years, the Middle East was the undisputed center of human civilization. The region is the birthplace of several of the world's major religions, and for centuries its achievements in science and the arts outshone those of the rest of the world. However, in recent decades this region has experienced much strife and conflict that threatens its future development and growth. Today, the non-Gulf Middle Eastern developing countries—Iraq, Jordan, Lebanon, Syria, and the Palestinian Territories, and Yemen*—are home to over 87 million people living at the crossroads between Europe, Asia, and Africa, between the Atlantic and Pacific Oceans, and bounded by the Indian Ocean and Mediterranean Sea. The region's location, climate, access to major transportation routes, and natural resources have resulted in a turbulent history; the ebb and flow of conquering nations, coupled with widespread internal conflict, over time have diminished the intellectual leadership and strength that the region once possessed.

In spite of unpredictable and often disruptive conditions, these countries have steadily and actively sought to develop their educational systems. Middle Easterners have historically placed a high value on education at all levels, and today gaining the best possible education remains an essential goal in many families. Although the region has recently witnessed several efforts to reestablish its former competitive position, these nations still struggle with reforming their various educational sectors. Public and pri-

---

* We have limited our sample to the non-Gulf countries of the Middle East, further narrowing down the selection based on countries' GDP per capita. Israel was not selected because of its relatively high GDP per capita.

vate institutions have in many cases undertaken major initiatives to meet the emerging challenges confronting their countries. Concerned individuals in these countries strongly believe that only through the full development of their higher education ministries and institutions can these countries once again become competitive world leaders. The full development of human capital represents the foundation of their future.

The Importance Strategic Planning in Higher Education in the Region

Situated in the heart of the Middle East and North Africa (MENA) region, Iraq, Jordan, Lebanon, the Palestinian Territories, Syria, and Yemen present cases that are quite different, particularly when compared to neighboring Gulf countries. Although both groups are facing a number of common challenges in their higher education sectors, Gulf countries can mobilize their considerable wealth to effect change, while non-Gulf countries must confront the added barriers of ongoing conflict and a paucity of resources (Salehi-Isfahani & Dhillon, 2008).

The non-Gulf countries share a number of social and economic trends that have presented many obstacles to their development, particularly in the education sector. Economic instability is one of the most critical challenges facing most of these nations today. In order to address these economic difficulties, non-Gulf countries have long relied on remittance economies, sending many youth abroad to work and receiving local economic returns. However, with the escalation of the global economic crisis, this economic strategy has been severely strained. Although these countries, with the exception of Iraq, do not produce oil, they have been greatly impacted by the downturn of the economic situation of the MENA region at large, and the Gulf countries in particular, since the non-Gulf countries are leading exporters of skilled and semi-skilled labor to the oil-producing countries. Additionally, the youth population of the non-Gulf region is growing rapidly; it is estimated that youth ages 15–24 represent one-third of the region's population. The high level of unemployment as a consequence of economic downturn, coupled with the high growth rate of the youth population, has led to major social and economic challenges (Salehi-Isfahani & Dhillon, 2008).

In addition to these challenges, most of these countries are facing great threats to human security. Threats range from political instability to local strife and civil wars that jeopardize one of the most critical sectors for development: education. Concerns about human security draw the attention and resources of governments away from education, especially when higher education is viewed as accruing private returns to individuals and their families. Higher education development is unquestionably one of the most effective potential responses to economic and social crisis in the non-Gulf developing countries. However, without organized and coordinated planning, these efforts may not yield the gains sought. Quality planning both within and among institutions is needed to address the needs of these societies. But in order to understand present challenges, we must first explore the significant growth and development that has taken place in higher education over the past few decades in each nation.

Overview of National Higher Education Systems

Iraq

Iraq is well known for its long and proud tradition of distinguished universities. However, its education system has been severely damaged by the series of wars and sanctions the country has endured in the past three decades. Most of Iraq's higher education infrastructure has been destroyed, and many academics have been lost through faculty assassinations and ongoing threats.

The modern history of Iraq's rich higher education system dates back to 1957, when the University of Baghdad was founded (Ministry of Higher Education and Scientific Research, 2009). To meet the growing demand for equity and access to higher education, additional higher education institutions were established, and today Iraq's higher education system consists of 20 universities and 47 technical institutes under the management of the Ministry of Higher Education and Scientific Research (MHESR). Most students are enrolled in universities in Baghdad, with women representing 42 percent of the students (UNESCO, 2004). The country's higher education system faces a number of challenges particular to Iraq, among which are the widespread destruction of the infrastructure of the higher education system, lack of reliable sources of utilities, an unstable and dangerous environment for normal academic activity, deteriorating quality of education (particularly heightened at times of sanctions, which isolated the local academic community from international academic communities), deteriorating levels of professionals and academic staff, poorly equipped labs, and a rapidly growing student population. Although there is still no dedicated national budget for higher education in Iraq, ad hoc amounts are regularly allocated. In such an unstable context, planning is a challenging task. Contingency alternatives to assist and improve the Iraqi higher education system have been proposed at a number of national and international meetings, but to date they have not been implemented. It is imperative for a country like Iraq to invest in its human capital and human development in order to generate sustainable socioeconomic development.

Jordan

Unlike Iraq, Jordan has enjoyed a considerable period of stability, which has helped to advance higher education in the country. The beginning of the higher education system in the country was marked by the founding of a number of teachers' colleges in the 1960s, and by the establishment of the first public Jordanian university, the University of Jordan, in 1962. In response to the need for regulation and planning of higher education policies and coordination among Jordanian public universities, the Jordanian Council of Higher Education was established in 1982. The council was one of the first steps towards establishing the Ministry of Higher Education and Scientific Research in 1985. In 1989, the Council of Higher Education endorsed the first policy document authorizing the establishment of private universities. The Ministry was dissolved in 1998, but reopened in 2001. The new Ministry supervises all higher education issues in the country, encompassing the Higher Education Council, the Accreditation Commission, and the Higher Committee for Scientific Research. The Ministry oversees the programs offered by both private and public institutions and evaluates their effectiveness in implementing the vision, mission, and objectives of higher education in the country. Currently, there are 8 public and 13 private universities in Jordan (Ministry of Higher Education and Scientific Research, 2009). Despite the continuous support of the Jordanian government for the country's higher education sector, high rates of youth unemployment persist in a country where more and more families are seeking to further their children's education through investments in university education.

Lebanon

Since its foundation in 1866, the Lebanese higher education sector has been growing and evolving, reflecting both the country's development and its educational needs. Prior to the establishment of the first public university in Lebanon, missionaries established and supported a number of private higher education institutions. It was not until the 1950s that the first and only public university was founded. The first Ministry of Education in Lebanon was established in 1955 with the goal of regulating the education sector in the country, and the Directorate General for Higher Education at the Ministry currently oversees the higher education sector. Despite the country's 15-year civil war, several private institutions were founded, and the number of institutions grew particularly rapidly during the 1990s. Today, there are 27 universities present in Lebanon, including one national university (Ministry of Education and Higher Education, 2009). While private institutions do not directly report to the Ministry and the Ministry does not control private institutions, there exists a long-standing, informal relationship between the Ministry and these institutions that permits them to enjoy total autonomy of governance and at the same time to maintain a liaison role that facilitates communication and cooperation (El-Ghali et al., 2010). The war caused massive damage to the higher education sector in Lebanon, but the large amount of growth the country witnessed both in terms of student enrollments and the number of universities in less than 10 years has brought a great deal of attention to this sector. Despite these private investments in higher education, Lebanon still faces chronic crises of youth unemployment and brain drain. In addition to the ongoing loss of human capital, the country is in a constant state of political and economic instability, which has greatly impacted universities. Planning thus becomes a challenging task, fraught with social, economic, and political challenges and a high level of uncertainty and risk.

Palestinian Territories

As in Lebanon, the Palestinian Territories suffer from a high level of political instability and a continuous state of uncertainty. In a country where resources are quite limited, higher education plays a vital role in the Palestinian Territories' social, political, and economic development. Furthermore, Palestinians place a high value on higher education because of their worldwide population dispersion (Zatari & Soltan, 2002). Due to the political situation that the Palestinians have been living through for the past few decades, they have spread throughout the world and adopted education as a major tool for survival in the absence of social security mechanisms. Although many Palestinians have fled for security reasons, they still maintain connections to the Palestinian Territories, as shown by the remittance economy that remains a primary survival mechanism. The educated members of the Palestinian diaspora have not relinquished their Palestinian identity.

The higher education system in the Palestinian Territories consists of colleges, universities, research centers, vocational training centers, and continuing education centers. It is composed of 10 universities, 14 community colleges, and 3 university colleges (Ministry of Education and Higher Education, 2005). Although the higher education sector began to emerge in the Palestinian Territories in the early 1950s, the official Ministry of Education, which became the Ministry of Education and Higher Education (MOEHE) in 2002, was not established until 1994. The MOEHE directly oversees the country's public universities (Hashweh & Hashweh, 1999). Despite the many difficulties facing the higher education sector in the country, student enrollment has continued to rise, with 55 percent of those enrolled in higher education attending traditional universities (Ministry of Education and Higher Education, 2005). The comprehensive internal closure and siege that have been progressively imposed on the Palestinian Territories as a result of the internal conflict with Israel led to the isolation of Palestinian cities from each other, and thus restricted the movement of students, staff, and others. This created serious obstacles for universities and their management, limiting academic development and hindering the exchange of resources between local higher education institutions (Zatari & Soltan, 2002). In addition to the resulting isolation, the deteriorating economic situation in the Territories rendered many Palestinian students unable to pay their tuition and other fees to the universities, which eventually led to high dropout rates. Finally, the higher education system in the Palestinian Territories suffers from academic brain drain, as evidenced by the shortages of faculty in specialized areas such as engineering and computers. In the hope of addressing these challenges, the MOEHE has put together a five-year strategic plan for the sector.

Syria

Over the past half century, the higher education system in Syria has been dominated by public institutions. It was not until 2001 that the Syrian government began licensing private universities. Today, Syria has nine private universities in addition to the five state-controlled public universities. The Council for Higher Education, which consists of representatives of universities, teachers, and students, and of the ministries of education, health, planning, and higher education, is responsible for the overall policy concerning teaching and scientific research in the country (Ministry of Higher

Education, 2004). In addition to the newly introduced concept of private universities, other relatively novel phenomena such as cost sharing initiatives and curricular upgrades also accompanied higher education reform in Syria (Kabbani & Salloum, 2009). This has led to a decrease in public spending and a consequent increase in private spending on higher education. Enrollment in higher education increased as a result of these reform efforts, although public institutions continue to enroll the most students. Most of the students enrolled at universities in Syria major in social sciences and humanities, which has led to high rates of unemployment among educated youth, reflecting a lack of awareness of the labor market needs in the country (Wahed, 2009).

In 2002, the Ministry of Higher Education launched a project in collaboration with the United Nations Development Programme to establish a network connecting the Syrian universities, the Syrian Higher Education Research Network (SHERN), in hopes that the network would lead to the development of academic applications such as distance learning, courseware content sharing and development, academic teleworking, and scientific research (Ministry of Higher Education, 2004). Despite these reform efforts and innovations, the higher education sector in Syria still faces major challenges, including meeting the increasing demand for higher education and the tendency of the system to inhibit creative thinking at universities (which is often ascribed to an excessive emphasis on rote learning and memorization). As with other countries in the region, Syria is facing an unemployment crisis among educated youth. Although the country has the financial resources needed to address most of its higher education challenges through planning, the scarcity of local expertise, the resistance to change at all levels, and the lack of awareness of the benefits of these reforms place the sector in a rather stagnant state (Ministry of Education, 2004).

Yemen

The situation in Yemen is similar to the situation in neighboring countries. Although the higher education sector witnessed an expansion in the 1990s, there are only seven public and four private universities in Yemen today. Prior to 1962, Yemeni students who aspired to pursue higher education had no choice but to travel to neighboring countries for university study (Selvaratnam & Regel, 1991). In 1970, the Yemeni government established the first public university by upgrading a teacher training institute. Recently, the Ministry of Higher Education and Scientific Research threatened to shut down all the private universities because they still do not have final licenses from the government. The Ministry is demanding that all private universities currently holding preliminary licenses comply with certain legal requirements in order to maintain these licenses. One of the Ministry's requirements is that universities reformulate their planning efforts and missions to include specific objectives designed to meet Yemen's development needs.

In addition to the current constraints within the country's higher education sector, Yemen is experiencing a significant student enrollment problem. Currently, less than 10 percent of secondary school graduates enroll in university study (Ministry of Higher

Chapter Four | Hana A. El-Ghali, Qianyi Chen, John L. Yeager
STRATEGIC PLANNING IN HIGHER EDUCATION IN THE MIDDLE EAST

Education and Scientific Research, 2005). This may very well change with the expected rise in Yemen's youth population. Along with the enrollment crisis, Yemen also faces the recurrent problem of unemployment among educated youth. According to the Ministry of Higher Education and Scientific Research (2005), factors hindering the development of the higher education sector include severe constraints on the ability of individual universities to make decisions on the allocation of funds and poor governance in the higher education system. As a result, the Ministry has addressed the country's higher education problems in its strategic plan for the development of the sector (Ministry of Higher Education and Scientific Research, 2005).

Study Methodology and Information Sources

Each of the non-Gulf countries is facing unique challenges, in addition to common regional difficulties that are particularly formidable in light of severe global economic distress and chronic regional political tensions. These conditions reinforce the need for universities to put forth an effort to maximize the utilization of scarce resources through effective planning. To understand the current status of institutional strategic planning in these developing countries, the authors conducted an initial study of the status of planning activities at universities in six Middle Eastern counties: Iraq, Jordan, Lebanon, the Palestinian Territories, Syria, and Yemen. For this purpose, the authors developed a database of strategic planning activities at higher education institutions in the region using three information sources: the websites of the respective government higher education bodies in each country, websites of higher education institutions, and a survey of selected institutions. The study initially identified and examined the published websites of all universities in these countries, a total of 90 institutions. The study examined each institution's website for information related to the development of institutional strategic planning activities. Based on this assessment, three universities from each country were invited to participate in a survey addressing their preparation of a strategic institutional plan.

One of the study's limitations was that considerable data were lacking at both the national and institutional levels. An examination of institutional websites revealed that many colleges and universities may not have developed strategic plans. Alternatively, they may have developed strategic plans but not chosen to publish information about them. The authors also examined available institutional websites for supplemental information that would support other evidence attesting to the existence of planning activities, such as the existence of a planning office or an institutional research office. Although not an absolute indicator of planning, the presence of these units within the university would suggest some level of institutional planning awareness.

Based on available information derived from the database, the study developed a regional summary of institutional higher education strategic planning activities. This provided an overview of the status of planning in the higher education sector across these developing countries.

Study Results

Individual institutional strategic planning activities are key to the development of a fully integrated higher education sector. The following section will examine major trends identified through an examination of websites and institutional survey results. The analysis integrates findings from both methods to provide a better understanding of the current status of these universities' planning activities. The findings from the six countries are presented and discussed together to provide a regional perspective on higher education planning in non-Gulf Middle Eastern countries.

Website Survey

The 90 universities in these six countries provided the population for this study. Out of this population, 76 institutions had English-language websites and 55 institutions had at least one of the major components of a strategic plan, defined by the project as external and internal assessments, vision/mission statements, goals/objectives, and strategies. Of these components, the mission statement appeared most frequently on the university websites reviewed for the project, although a number of institutions also included an analysis of strengths, weaknesses, opportunities, and threats (SWOT). A number of institutions indicated that they have a planning office, department, or committee. Only 9 universities of the 76 institutions had published their strategic plans online. Most of the published plans were complete, including major components.

As might be expected, institutions in different countries are at different stages of developing their higher education strategic plans. For example, strategic planning practices seemed to be relatively common in certain countries like Lebanon, the Palestinian Territories, and Jordan, and less evident in other countries such as Syria and Yemen. Despite this observation, ministries of higher education in the various countries have provided information on strategic planning efforts, such as the five-year plans of Iraq and the Palestinian Territories published online. This observation was true, with the exception of Yemen. The government of Yemen mapped out a thorough strategic plan with all essential elements, and the plan has been published online by the country's Ministry of Higher Education. Other countries, like Lebanon, also had a Ministry-developed strategic plan, which was shared with the researchers of this study upon request.

Survey Results

To gain an understanding of how these institutions perceive trends affecting their national higher education sectors, the researchers distributed an opened-ended query to gain a deeper understanding of institutional planning within each country. Over 50 percent of responding institutions (six institutions) indicated that they had conducted formal reviews of external trends within the last four years. Most institutions updated these reviews every two to five years, indicating that they recognized the importance of continuous assessment of external trends. Institutions were requested to list the most important current educational and social trends that they perceived were facing the higher education sector in their respective countries. Institutional responses covered many issues, which are grouped into several categories in table 4.1: resources, students, academic quality, curricula/programs, politics/society, and others.

TABLE 4.1: EXAMPLES OF EXTERNAL ISSUES AND TRENDS IN STRATEGIC PLANNING

Resources	Capacity building
	Lack of scientific labs, equipment, and resources
	Shortage of budget for higher education institutions
	High cost of education at most private higher education institutions
	Lack of trained faculty and staff
	Demand for education professionals
Students	Increase in the number of unemployed university graduates
	Increase in enrollment in higher education
	Increase in competition among universities for students
	Lack of access to higher education
Academic Quality	Lack of coordination between K–12 education and higher education
	Proliferation of institutions claiming more than what they can deliver
	Excessive emphasis on marketable degrees and programs, often at the expense of academic rigor
	Accreditation (particularly through international agencies)
	Growth of quality assurance of programs
	Increase in calls for education accountability
Curricula/Programs	Need for emphasis on English learning
	Increased demand for improved research skills
	Increase in the dominance of technology
	Increase in the improvement of computer and IT skills
Politics/Society	Educational reform including autonomy for universities
	Instability of the philosophy and methods of education and strong political influence over the higher education sector
	Increased political instability resulting in security concerns
	Excessive politicization of the universities
	Laissez-faire mode of governance at the state level leading to the rapid and chaotic expansion of the private sector
	Graduates' social mobility
	Linkage of education and social and economic goals
	Students' educational mobility
Other Issues	Students' improved communication using a foreign language, such as English and/or French

The trends depicted in table 4.1 are a sample of the changes confronting higher education in these countries. A number of issues and trends cutting across the countries have led to common challenges and opportunities for the universities in the region. To address these challenges, private institutions have begun to engage in institutional strategic planning activities. Almost all of the responding institutions have developed multi-year plans within the last five years, and half of these institutions have established planning offices to coordinate their activities. Many respondents indicated that the primary motivation for developing or revising their plans was changing external trends (55 percent). Other reasons for changing institutional plans included a change in leadership, changing internal conditions (such as a need to increase institutional quality), and changes in the institution's mission. In general, these planning initiatives have taken place under the direction of the governing board and the university's leadership.

The reporting institutions indicated that most of the plans (approximately 70 percent) contained major elements typically found in strategic plans worldwide: external and internal assessment, vision/mission statement, goals/objectives, and strategies. Although written copies of plans were not available in all cases, most institutional plans reportedly examined a range of issues and considered a comprehensive array of planning elements.

Major goals of these institutional planning activities focused on areas such as alignment of curriculum with market needs, desire to become a world-class institution, enhancement of the quality of all institutional programs, selective program development, improvement of university management, and increased efficiency of administrative performance. In addition, each responding institution provided various strategies they would use to meet these goals. Examples of strategies corresponding to the major goals include but are not limited to:

- Identifying the skills, tools, and knowledge that should be possessed by the graduates to meet the requirements of the labor markets;
- Supporting internationalization by expanding study abroad programs, offering language and cultural immersion opportunities for faculty and staff, providing funds for international travel, etc.;
- Increasing faculty membership in certain fields in order to provide additional capacity that contributes to international scholarship;
- Reviewing and improving existing programs, and establishing new programs.
- Strengthening the quality of human resources, especially the quality of faculty;
- Implementing comprehensive enrollment programs to increase the number, quality, and diversity of students;
- Expanding the physical plant; and
- Implementing or expanding information technology structure to increase administrative efficiency.

It is evident from an examination of the individual institutional survey results that these institutions clearly understood the needs of their societies, in addition to their own specific institutional needs, and that they were in the process of developing appropriate responses. In most cases, the institutions conducted external reviews to identify societal needs, such as the shortage in budgets dedicated for higher education, an increase in calls for education accountability, and the need for emphasis on English learning. These plans do represent a response on the part of these higher education institutions to the needs of their societies, but they lack the kind of cohesive, unified planning framework that could be provided by strong leadership at the level of the institution or a potential consortium.

When respondents were asked about the reasons for poor implementation or lack of implementation of plans, they elaborated on a number of issues: national instability, political polarization, employee motivation, lack of management information, lack of funding, lack of available staff, weak commitment from senior staff, resistance to change from faculty and staff, and centralized decision making. These reasons are similar to those found in the literature addressing why plans are often not fully implemented in international settings (Presley and Leslie, 1999; Rowley and Sherman, 2001; Alfred, 2006). The inability of institutions to successfully implement new plans in response to changing internal and external conditions weakens the country's ability to develop and improve its higher education sector, therefore potentially having a negative impact on each country's economic, social, and political development (Peterson et al., 1997).

Although many institutions reported that their plans had not been implemented or that they had not yet identified ways to implement their plans, many did report that planning had led to positive results. Examples of some of the successes attributed to institutional planning were: new recruiting strategies resulting in improved enrollments; new mission statements; establishment of new academic programs; establishment of new research programs; better implementation of the annual curriculum for initial studies and higher education; improved quality assurance processes; improvement of enrollment and hiring practices; implementation of new IT systems; development of new funding sources such as external giving campaigns; and improved infrastructure and physical plant. Moreover, most of the participating institutions (78 percent) had an evaluation process in place for assessing their institutional strategic planning.

It is essential to note that among the limitations of this study is the relatively low participation in the open-ended query that was submitted to the universities in the sample countries. Only two institutions from Iraq, Lebanon, and the Palestinian Territories responded to the survey. However, this is also significant, for these countries have experienced particularly high levels of political instability and armed conflict in the past few years.

To a large extent, the survey results are consistent with the results of the web research. Data from the website overview and survey results show that in the absence of strong regional or national planning efforts, several institutions initiated their own strategic plans in order to address the needs of their societies. However, it cannot be concluded with certainty that universities that did not respond to the survey or did not have strategic plans published on their websites have not engaged in planning activities. It is evident that some institutions in the region have identified major internal and external issues and trends, and have set strategic goals to address related challenges and opportunities.

Comments on the Prospects of Institutional Strategic Planning

If a university invests its scarce resources in developing an institutional strategic plan, it makes sense to share that plan with others to demonstrate cutting-edge management practices and distribute information that may be of value in developing cooperative activities (Bryson, 1995). The information reviewed from country and university websites, in conjunction with the institutional survey results, indicated that most institutions had a number of ambitious educational initiatives that they believed important to address, and the authors found great deal of similarity and overlap. These initiatives include:

- Strengthening human resources by providing faculty and staff training, retaining or vigorously recruiting qualified faculty and staff members;
- Strengthening or adding new academic programs, especially the graduate programs or those which address the needs of the society or market;
- Developing and implementing strong and comprehensive enrollment management programs to increase student population, diversity, and/or quality; and
- Diversifying sources of income to support academic change.

Further, most institutions indicated that a major barrier to implementing these initiatives was the lack of sufficient economic or human resources. Thus, institutions may be able to benefit from cooperative activities by pooling scarce resources to achieve shared goals.

These countries and institutions share many common historical, cultural, and religious roots. They also share many of the same problems, and cooperative activities could therefore potentially offer solutions applicable to many of these institutions. Based on our study of the websites and the institutional surveys, the following are illustrations of potential cooperative activities that could be addressed through partnerships or consortia:

Option 1—Enhanced electronic instructional systems could provide increased access to programming and an opportunity to reach more students. Specialized instructional programming could include foreign language instruction and science.

Option 2—Faculty and staff research programs could be developed to enhance and enrich institutional research capacity. Faculty could share research agendas, facilities, funding, skills, and knowledge.

Option 3—Multi-institutional faculty development programs could be designed and implemented, allowing development and presentation costs to be shared. Shared regional programming would help to develop greater understanding and cooperation between faculty of different institutions, and the development of new faculty capacities through the sharing of resources across institutions.

By sharing knowledge and skills, many institutions can expand their contributions not only to their own higher education institutions, but also to the region and the countries in which they operate.

Conclusion

A wide variety of human talent and resources is available at higher educational institutions in the non-Gulf Middle East. Although not all of these countries have an abundance of financial resources available for higher education, they have a wealth of human capital that needs to be fully developed and utilized. Because of these assets, Lebanon, for example, emerged from a 15-year civil war to remain among the leaders of higher education in the region. Many of the universities in these developing countries have invested in planning efforts in an attempt to better address their societies' needs and to respond to constantly fluctuating economic and political conditions. This study clearly found that most of these institutions are involved in some aspect of strategic planning. However, without coordinated efforts to organize these initiatives, national higher education systems may not be able to lead efforts to develop their institutions, their countries, or the region.

TABLE 4.2: LIST OF NON-GULF MIDDLE EASTERN UNIVERSITY WEBSITES SURVEYED

University	University Website
Iraq	
University of Baghdad	http://univofbaghdad.org/english_main/3.htm
Basrah University	http://members.lycos.co.uk/basrahuniversity/
University of Dohuk	http://uod.ac/index.php
University of Mosul	http://www.mosuluniversity.org/index_e.htm
University of Kufa	http://kuiraq.com/en/
University of Salahaddin	http://www.suh.ac/
Jordan	
University of Jordan	http://www.ju.edu.jo/
Yarmouk University	http://portal.yu.edu.jo/
Jordan University of Science and Technology	http://www.just.edu.jo/
Hashemite University	http://www.hu.edu.jo/
Philadelphia University	http://www.philadelphia.edu.jo/university/
Mu'tah University	http://www.mutah.edu.jo/
Applied Science University	http://www.aspu.edu.jo/
Al-Balqa Applied University	http://www.aabfs.org/English/EnIndex.asp?
Al al-Bayt University	http://www.bau.edu.jo/
University of Petra	http://www.aabu.edu.jo/
Al-Isra Private University	http://www.uop.edu.jo/
Al-Zaytoonah Private University of Jordan	http://www.isra.edu.jo/en/
German-Jordanian University	http://www.alzaytoonah.edu.jo/ZaySite/pages/En/Main.aspx
Zarqa Private University	http://www.gju.edu.jo/default.aspx?lang=en
Princess Sumaya University of Technology	http://english.zpu.edu.jo/
Al-Hussein Bin Talal University	http://www.psut.edu.jo/
Amman Arab University for Graduate Studies	http://www.aau.edu.jo/
Irbid National University	http://www.inu.edu.jo/
Al-Ahliyya Amman University	http://www.ammanu.edu.jo/
Jerash Private University	http://www.jpu.edu.jo/EN/home.php
Lebanon	
Lebanese University	http://www.ul.edu.lb/
American University of Beirut	http://www.aub.edu.lb/
Lebanese American University	http://www.lau.edu.lb/
Beirut Arab University	http://www.bau.edu.lb/
Saint Joseph University	http://www.usj.edu.lb/
Notre Dame University	http://www.ndu.edu.lb/
University of Balamand	http://www.balamand.edu.lb/
Holy Spirit University of Kaslik	http://www.usek.edu.lb/
University of Antonin	http://www.upa.edu.lb/
American University of Science & Technology	http://www.aust.edu.lb/

Al Jinan University	http://www.jinan.edu.lb/english/
Lebanese International University	http://www.liu.edu.lb/
Islamic University of Lebanon	http://www.iul.edu.lb/
Haigazian University	http://www.haigazian.edu.lb/
Global University	http://www.gu.edu.lb/
American University of Technology	http://www.aut.edu/
Sagesse University	http://www.uls.edu.lb/
Middle East University	http://www.meu.edu.lb/
Beirut Islamic University	http://www.biu.edu.lb/
Modern University for Business and Science	http://www.mubs.edu.lb/
Al-Manar University of Tripoli	http://www.mut.edu.lb/
Makassed University of Beirut	http://www.makassed.org/uni/index_uni.html
Lebanese French University of Technology and Applied Sciences	http://www.cut.edu.lb/
Lebanese German University	http://www.lgu.edu.lb/
Hariri Canadian University	http://www.hariricanadian.edu.lb/
Art Sciences & Technology University of Lebanon	http://www.aul.edu.lb/
Arab Open University	http://www.aou.edu.lb/aou/
Palestinian Territories	
The Islamic University of Gaza	http://www.iugaza.edu.ps/en/
Birzeit University	http://www.birzeit.edu/
Al-Quds University	http://www.alquds.edu/
Palestine Polytechnic University	http://www.ppu.edu/EnglishSite/
An-Najah National University	http://www.najah.edu/
Arab American University-Jenin	http://www.aauj.edu/AAUJ_site/index.php
Bethlehem University	http://www.bethlehem.edu/index.php
Hebron University	http://www.hebron.edu/
Al-Azhar University of Gaza	http://www.alazhar.edu.ps/
Palestine Technical College	http://www.ptcdb.edu.ps/ar/
Syria	
Damascus University	http://www.damasuniv.shern.net/
Tishreen University	http://www.tishreen.shern.net/new%20site/englishsite/index.htm
Al-Baath University	http://www.albaath-univ.edu.sy/
Higher Institute for Applied Science and Technology	http://www.hiast.edu.sy/en/
International University for Science and Technology	http://www.iust.edu.sy/index.php
University of Kalamoon	http://www.uok.edu.sy/
Wadi International University	http://www.wgsu.biz/
Ittihad University	http://www.ittihad.ac.ae/english_pages/index_e.htm
Private University of Science and Arts	http://www.pusa-sy.org/en/pusa.php
Al-Andalus University for Medical Sciences	http://www.au.edu.sy/english/
Arab International University	http://www.aiu.edu.sy/
Al-Hawash Private University for Pharmacy and Cosmetology	http://www.hpu.sy/en/index.php

Yemen	
Sana'a University	http://new.suye.ac/en/Default.aspx
University of Science and Technology Sana'a	http://www.ust.edu/ic/profiles1.html
Queen Arwa University	http://www.y.net.ye/arwauniversity/english/index.htm
Hodeidah University	http://www.hoduniv.edu.ye/
Al-Ahgaff University	http://www.ahgaff.edu/
Hadramout University of Science and Technology	http://www.hust.edu.ye/prochure.pdf
Ibb University	http://www.ibbunv.com.ye/1-Englesh.htm
National University	http://www.nationaluni.net/index.php
Sana'a University	http://new.suye.ac/en/Default.aspx
Al-Eman University	http://www.jameataleman.org/

Note: The following universities' websites were not available for review: Syria—University of Aleppo, Mamoon University for Science and Technology; Yemen—University of Aden.

REFERENCES

Alfred, R. L. (2006). *Managing the big picture in colleges and universities: From tactics to strategy*. Westport, CT: Praeger Publishers.

Bryson, J. M. (1995). *Strategic planning for public and nonprofit organizations: A guide to strengthening and sustaining organizational achievement*. San Francisco, CA: Jossey-Bass.

El-Ghali, H., Yeager, J. L., & Zein, Z. (2010). A policy framework for higher education in Lebanon: The role of strategic planning. In J. N. Hawkins & W. J. Jacob (Eds.), in *Policy debates in comparative, international, and development education*. New York, NY: Palgrave MacMillan.

Hashweh, M., & Hashweh, M. (1999). Higher education in Palestine: Current status and recent developments. *Mediterranean Journal of Educational Studies, 4*(2), 221–227.

Kabbani, N., & Salloum, S. (2009, June 17–18). *Financing higher education in Syria*. Paper presented at the Economic Research Forum Regional Conference on Financing Higher Education in Arab Countries, Amman, Jordan.

Ministry of Education and Higher Education. (2009). *Lebanese Ministry of Education and Higher Education*. Retrieved February 15, 2009 from http://www.higher-edu.gov.lb

Ministry of Education and Higher Education. (2005). *Palestinian Higher Education Statistics 2005*. Retrieved October 2009 from http://www.palestina.int.ar/Universidades/StatisticsHE.pdf

Ministry of Higher Education. (2004). *Syrian higher education system*. Retrieved October 2009 from http://www.mhe.gov.sy

Ministry of Higher Education and Scientific Research. (2009). *Iraqi Ministry of Higher Education and Scientific Research*. Retrieved October 2009 from http://www.mohesr.gov.iq/EngPages/indexE.htm

Ministry of Higher Education and Scientific Research. (2009). *Jordanian Ministry of Higher Education and Scientific Research*. Accessed October 2009 from http://www.mohe.gov.jo

Ministry of Higher Education and Scientific Research. (2005). *National strategy for the development of higher education in Yemen*. Retrieved October 2009 from http://www.hepyemen.org/en

Peterson, M. W., Dill, D. D., & Mets, L. A. (1997). *Planning and management for a changing environment: A handbook on redesigning postsecondary institutions*. San Francisco, CA: Jossey-Bass.

Presley, J. B., & Leslie, D. W. (1999). Understanding strategy: An assessment of theory and practice. In J. C. Smart (Ed.), *Higher education handbook of theory and research* (pp. 201–239). New York, NY: Agathon Press.

Rowley, D. J., & Sherman, H. (2001). *From strategy to change: Implementing the plan in higher education*. San Francisco, CA: Jossey-Bass.

Salehi-Isfahani, D., & Dhillon, N. (2008, October). *Stalled youth transitions in the Middle East: A framework for policy reform*. Washington, DC and Dubai, United Arab Emirates: The Wolfensohn Center for Development and The Dubai School of Government.

Selvaratnam, V., & Regel, O. L. (1991). *Higher education in the Republic of Yemen: The University of Sana'a*. Washington, DC: World Bank.

United Nations Educational, Scientific, and Cultural Organization (UNESCO). (2004). *Iraq, education in transition: Needs and challenges*. Paris, France: UNESCO.

Wahed, M. N. A. (2009, June 16–18). *ICT in higher education in Syria*. Paper presented at the Regional Follow-up to the Outcome of the World Summit on the Information Society, Damascus, Syria.

Zatari, D., & Soltan, A. (2002, Spring). Challenges facing higher education development in Palestine. *EAIE Forum*.

Chapter Five

THE ROLE OF INTERNATIONALIZATION IN WOMEN'S EDUCATION IN THE MIDDLE EAST

HAIFA REDA JAMAL AL-LAIL, PRESIDENT, EFFAT UNIVERSITY

Internationalization of higher education has given women in the Middle East numerous opportunities to connect with the international community without necessarily leaving "home." Increasingly, women throughout the Middle East are embracing international projects, initiatives, and agencies. They are beginning to directly shape international higher education experiences and communities, and thus are playing an important role in the development of internationalization. More significantly, they are also helping shape social and economic policy in their own nations.

In the Middle East, educators and policy makers must take into account the cultural framework of women's broadly perceived primary role as caregivers and providers (Li & Karakowsky, 2001). In the regional context, this concept should underlie internationalization efforts in general, and internationalization of women's higher education in particular, in order to guarantee better and more meaningful experiences for students and educators in the region and beyond.

This chapter discusses contemporary global innovations in the field of higher education, focusing on the internationalization of higher education in the Middle East. Specifically, it looks at the effect of internationalization on women's education and how this process impacts social and national development. The first part reviews trends in the internationalization of higher education, outlines its driving factors, and identifies implications for its growth and expansion in the Middle East. The second part reflects on how internationalization in the region affects women's advancement in higher education and beyond. The third part summarizes policy implications; explores the potential impact on social and economic development in the Middle East and beyond; and outlines the benefits that stem from internationalization, including broader educational and professional opportunities for women.

Trends in the Internationalization of Higher Education: A Review

Over the past 30 years, rapid advances in information technology have revolutionized the way universities operate nationally and internationally. Individual institutions of higher education are becoming more and more woven into an international sphere of activities and influence. The driving logic behind these internationalization efforts may include knowledge production and commercialization, personal ambition and aspiration, broadening awareness, cross-cultural understanding, building global networks, exchanging human and physical resources, or simply sharing experiences. These factors have provided a rationale for the emergence of new patterns of internationalization above and beyond the traditional "study abroad" model (Altbach, 2005, p. 1).

To survive and grow in this new world order, educational communities must pursue continuous integration and clustering with their counterparts around the world. This "clustering" should not be limited to the commonly accepted economic sense of the word, but instead should include convergence of diverse aims, policies, and practices—without sacrificing institutional individuality and uniqueness. This increasingly urgent need has yielded new forms of internationalization of higher education, ranging from study abroad programs to full-fledged overseas campuses to knowledge spaces, including knowledge cities and science parks that are new to the Middle East. These new patterns of internationalization in higher education are affecting different regions, countries and their populations, both male and female, in different ways (Altbach & Knight, 2006, p. 4–7). The cultural and social characteristics of the Middle East demand further development of this process of internationalization, with special attention to female advancement and empowerment.

Social, economic, political, and technological conditions in the Middle East have led many to view Western educational systems in general, and liberal arts institutions in particular, as the best models to improve educational quality (Eastwood, 2007; Ghabra & Arnold, 2007; Deghady, 2008; Rupp, 2009). Widespread esteem for the quality of such pedagogy made the adaptation of the women's liberal art college model to the Middle East seem not only a natural and inevitable phenomenon, but also beneficial at the national level. This is partially because the emergence of models for women's education in the West happened as a result of aims and conditions similar to those existing in the Middle East today. The early liberal arts colleges for women, particularly in the United States, were born out of a desire to provide quality education for women in order to ease their transition into society and the professions, while also striking a balance between modernity and their identity as women. In the Middle East in the second half of the 20th century, particularly on the Arabian Peninsula, similar conditions required that more women take part in the efforts of these societies to develop.

The broad extent of this social change is reflected in the fact that, in Saudi Arabia, some 36 percent of undergraduate women—and nearly 100 percent of those with master's degrees or doctorates—enter professions as widely diverse as teaching, medicine, and engineering (Al-Maimouni, 2009). The lower employment rate of bachelor's degree graduates is less the result of lack of opportunity than the consequence of a deliberate decision by many young women to devote themselves to family life to the exclusion of professional pursuits. However, the function and beneficial influence of those who, after graduation, elect to remain in a family environment must not be undervalued, since such women often play an influential role in the education of their children and offer intellectual support to their spouses.

Furthermore, the need for critical thinkers, basic technological skills, and civic engagement demanded significant reforms in education for women, as well as for men. Consequently, it was only natural that the earliest efforts to establish private colleges and universities for the education of women in the Middle East would be modeled after the liberal arts women's colleges in the West, and then eventually propelled forward in partnership with them.

Pioneering efforts and partnerships between Middle Eastern and Western countries planted seeds that eventually led to the growth of more homegrown concepts, forms, and methodologies for liberal arts education in the region. Over time, this translated into more and more high-quality educational options for women and opportunities to be exposed to international education and ideas without leaving home, although this in itself falls short of a full international experience (Gutierrez, Hawthorne, Kirk, & Powers, 2009, p. 8).

These new models of higher education in the Middle East, while beneficial, conceptualize internationalization primarily as a systemic flow of students, faculty, programs, knowledge, and institutions across borders in one direction. They also assume that this flow will embrace the cultural and social norms of traditional society as an important component in the design, structure, and function of these institutions. One example is the choice to be either in a co-ed environment, or in a segregated institution with the technologies necessary to communicate and collaborate with peers to accomplish necessary tasks.

These models also assumed that women and men would benefit equally from such a flow as long as the institutions adopted the internationalization policies in their current plans. These assumptions discouraged policy makers from promoting the development of a more two-way exchange. There were no incentives or scholarship programs to encourage Western women to experience life in the Middle East like those that most Middle Eastern countries have adopted for male and female students abroad since the 1960s and '70s. Social and cultural policies of the day were equally ineffective in attracting Western women to pursue international experiences in the region. Even to the present day, higher education institutions in the Middle East do not possess and have not even tried to create any customized degree or research programs to attract women from Western countries to come and study in their institutions. The main reason for this is a general reluctance among Westerners to accept living in a cultural environment that is often mistakenly perceived as restrictive. One must note that what in the West may be looked on as unduly restrictive is not viewed as such in Islamic culture. Indeed, most young Middle Eastern women feel more secure and comfortable when veiled, and more liberated in an exclusively female educational environment.

The result has been that relatively few Western and Middle Eastern women have been part of exchange experiences in the past, and these few women have not been sufficient to dispel faulty stereotypes on both sides in favor of a wider understanding of cultural and social differences. Most of the universities worldwide that have embraced internationalization strategies have applied them without first thinking through the importance of designing and adopting universal protocols to govern roles, responsibilities, activities, and degrees of influence between international stakeholders. The absence of globally applied principles or universal protocols to govern such exchanges has resulted in the emergence of various models customized to fit the needs of individual institutions. Thus, no internationally recognized standards have emerged to promote two-directional exchanges or to guarantee minimum numbers, degrees of compliance, and obligations from participants in such programs.

In 2004, The Organization for Economic Co-operation and Development (OECD) published a policy brief titled "Internationalization of Higher Education." The publication outlined the current position of the organization and set out an agenda for different policy rationales and approaches to cross-border education. The conclusion of the policy brief stresses the importance of a coherent policy that encompasses many stakeholders and policy areas with an effective policy strategy that takes into account diversity while ensuring the highest coordination, or compatibility, between several policy agendas, such as quality assurance and recognition, development assistance in education, other domestic educational policies, and policies related to culture, migration, visas, trade, and the economy.

The OECD initiative is a valuable foundation, and many researchers are now examining it in more detail from cultural, social, and economic points of view, in addition to the educational point of view. This research shows us that there is still much to be done to achieve optimum levels of compatibility with regard to such matters, including acknowledged standards and degree recognition, quality assurance and control, recognition of differing cultural and social norms, economic disparities, national priorities, and so forth (OECD, 2004, p. 7).

This chapter stresses the need to accept the cultural and social norms of inherently traditional family structures in the Middle East when promoting both internationalization of higher education in general, and internationalization of female higher education in particular. In order to promote internationalization of higher education in the Middle East, special attention should be given to the socioeconomic conditions that influence the extent to which women are integrated in the process. Addressing these issues will help to clarify the overall concept, and consequently contribute to future policies and research on the internationalization of higher education.

Internationalization of Higher Education and the Advancement of Women in the Middle East

The original concept of international education in the Muslim World stemmed from the mission of Muslims—both men and women—to fulfill their duty in life to pursue and search for knowledge, wherever in the world it might be. This mission resulted in the foundation of formal institutions of education by the Prophet Muhammad (peace be upon him) himself, who sat in the mosque surrounded by a *halqa* (circle) of listeners, intent on his instruction. The Prophet Muhammad relied heavily on sending teachers to the various tribes to instruct them in the text of the Holy Qur'an, which stressed the duty to study widely. Consequently, the pursuit of education flourished widely throughout the Arab world, leading to early examples of internationalization. The world's oldest continuously operating academic degree-granting university, the University of Al-Karaouine, was founded by a woman named Fatima Fihriyya in Morocco in the 9th century, and the second-oldest, Al-Azhar University, was founded in Egypt in the 10th century. These two institutions played a leading role in the cultural and academic relations between the Islamic world and Europe in the Middle Ages, producing numerous scholars who strongly influenced the intellectual and academic history of the Muslim and Western worlds. Their influence continues to be felt through scores of similarly structured universities throughout Europe and beyond.

Women were either completely absent from these developments or their participation was undocumented. This, no doubt, was because a woman's education in the Middle East has traditionally either been focused on her education as a mother or viewed as secondary to more important practical domestic priorities. This is due to the prevailing cultural attitude in most Arab societies that a woman's primary place in life is at home, and that the male should be the breadwinner.

Education for women in the Middle East did not progress at the same rate as education for men. There were no girls' schools in the region until the beginning of the 19th century, when foreign missionaries opened them for men and women in Egypt, Syria, and Lebanon. By the end of the century there were native as well as foreign schools, but women did not enter the universities of the Middle East until the late 1920s. Until many countries in the Middle East became independent from their former colonial governments, educational opportunities for girls were very limited.

These different factors meant that private higher education appeared in some countries earlier than in others, and this explains the presence of well-known private, nonprofit foreign universities such as the American University Beirut (AUB), founded in Lebanon in 1866, and the American University in Cairo (AUC), founded in Egypt in 1919 (Rupp, 2009, p. 2).

Eventually, the social and economic situation in almost all countries in the Middle East, except the Gulf countries, necessitated the entry of more and more women into the work force. Especially after independence, education for girls became a priority and was recognized as a way for a nation to utilize the full capacity of its human resources and to advance on the international scene (Deloitte, 2009).

At different times from the 1960s to the 1980s, most countries changed their policies. These changes ranged from compulsory primary and secondary education to different scholarship programs and privatization policies (El-Sanabary, 1992). Women benefitted greatly from these policies, but these benefits and gains did not match those of their male counterparts.

The roots for this rapid development are well established. Many countries made primary education compulsory for both boys and girls as their educational systems developed. The governments of most Middle Eastern countries pursued the privatization of education in the middle of the 20th century, encouraging private-sector involvement in the provision of education to meet demand for education in general, and higher education in particular. The drop in oil prices and the subsequent drop in the income of the Gulf states in the late 1980s advanced the privatization of education in those countries. Privatization initiatives were primarily undertaken to provide a faster response to perceived market trends. A complementary factor was the resulting introduction of experienced foreign academics.

Privatization motivated higher education providers to embrace internationalization as an important way to distinguish themselves from state universities. This required the inclusion of concepts such as diversity, interdisciplinary studies, intercultural experiences, and gender equality in the educational services they provided. These dimensions were very important survival factors for such institutions, serving not only to increase enrollments but also to ensure that male and female graduates received quality educations that could provide them with the global knowledge and skills needed by the international community in an increasingly competitive world (Al-Qazzat, 1980; Jamal, 2004; United Nations Development Programme, 2005).

Although it is still common to hear people express the view that it is more important for a boy to be educated than it is for a girl, recent educational reforms not only reinforced the idea of compulsory primary and secondary education for women; they also required that women's higher education be a key element in human capital development, enabling women to make a more effective contribution to the socioeconomic development of the region. Hand in hand, governments and private-sector organizations in the Middle East have designated improving the quality of higher education as an important step toward future development (World Bank, 2007a; World Bank, 2009).

As part of the internationalization process, different American and British models of higher education came to the region either in partnership with the locals or as a form of foreign direct investment in the region. These different models had different goals and agendas, ranging from small colleges, such as Effat University, to comprehensive research universities, such as the King Abdullah University of Science and Technology (KAUST) in Saudi Arabia, to complete educational cities, for example in Qatar or Dubai. All of these follow Western educational models with regard to pedagogy, structure, and student life. Some of these institutions and initiatives are still trying to strike a balance between cultural restrictions and Western models, and some have adopted the Western model in its entirety without looking adequately at cultural requirements. The result is a diverse combination that gives the people the ability to choose the institution or program that fits their needs. In these combinations, one sees that some of these institutions are exclusively for women, while others are coeducational with some segregation of male campuses and female campuses, and still others are completely coeducational, to match the varying stages of social and economic transformation taking place in the region. Rather ironically, the desire of many conservative families to provide international quality education for their daughters without permitting them to leave their countries of residence has been instrumental in facilitating the emergence of high-quality colleges in the Gulf region offering higher education options for women. These institutions include those located in Education City in Qatar, New York University (NYU) Abu Dhabi, and Zayed University in UAE, to name just a few. Effat University and Prince Sultan University were founded in Saudi Arabia—the region's most conservative state.

The exposure of women in the Middle East to international higher education abroad came gradually, especially for women from the Arabian Peninsula. In the early days, international experience in education came mostly as a result of a woman accompanying a male guardian who was himself studying abroad. Consequently, the opportunities for international experience abroad in higher education for women were limited to those fortunate enough to have a male guardian who was part of a scholarship program, and who himself supported the education of women. Those who were not fortunate enough to have these opportunities had no other options for international experience in higher education. This situation has, however, changed over the course of time. In recent years, the changes have been more drastic, due to advances in informational and educational technologies, which have opened new doors for the international education of women everywhere, and particularly in the Middle East. Different programs between Middle Eastern and Western universities have been developed and customized to fit the cultural values that restrict women in the Middle East from pursuing higher education. An example is the joint supervision programs that were established between King Abdul Aziz University in Saudi Arabia and a group of UK universities in the 1990s, which do not require that students be in the UK during their graduate studies.

The late 1990s and the early years of the 21st century have witnessed drastic changes. Women in the Gulf states, and everywhere in the Middle East, now have more choices and fewer restrictions in their pursuit of higher education. Women can now travel abroad and be full-time students in any Western university. Women can also study anywhere in the Middle East at international campuses that have been established in the region. These campuses allow a woman to benefit from a degree of international experience while staying at home, if she wishes to balance her family life and career opportunities. This option is largely a matter of personal preference rather than a concession to any perceived gender issue.

For women in the Middle East, the developments described above now offer numerous opportunities and choices to connect with the international community without necessarily leaving "home." Statistics show that more and more women are now able to be part of international programs and campuses, or to get internationally recognized degrees online, and indeed are taking advantage of such opportunities in ever-greater numbers. Such programs are now widely available throughout the Middle

East. However, these welcome developments are only part of the whole story of how women in the region are increasingly embracing different international projects, efforts, and agencies. Consequently, women are beginning to directly shape international higher education experiences and communities, and thus are playing a significant role in the development of internationalization.

A pamphlet titled "Arab Women in Public Life and Decision-Making," issued by the Economic and Social Commission for Western Asia (ESCWA) in 2006, offers a major review of the participation of women in public life in Arab countries and provides some evidence of progress made in various areas. These include gender equality, voting rights, participation of women in elections, the number of women holding ministerial and legislative seats, women's representation in local councils and municipalities, women's affiliation with political parties, involvement of women in the judiciary system, women's appointment to high-ranking and official posts, the role of women in the media, and the participation of women in civil society through nongovernmental organizations (NGOs) and other organizations. The pamphlet explores these issues via examples drawn from a variety of countries and situations. This review presents a clear situational analysis and guidelines as an essential step toward building a supportive and enabling environment for women in leadership positions.

Conclusions and Policy Implications

Women in the Middle East, and the communities to which they belong, have benefited considerably from internationalization in higher education. Furthermore, improvements in coordination not only increase the availability of women qualified to follow a profession with a potential international dimension, thus ultimately enriching society, but also greatly increase the prospects of integration in the work force, specifically for women in the Arab world. Consequently, international education gives women the possibility to move up the employment ladder, which leads to personal gains as well as wider social benefits.

Recognizing the need to work within the cultural framework of the Middle East, together with sound and effective implementation of programs, ensures that programs will be accepted by people in the region, especially women. Such recognition tends to generate further demand for strategies that take account of local culture. This cultural framework is an important ingredient of the socioeconomic development of the Middle East. Without recognizing this fundamental fact, the strategic goals of the internationalization of higher education are unattainable. This assumption is the key, not only to broaden women's opportunities in the Middle East, but also to guarantee meaningful internationalization of higher education worldwide.

Certainly, there are individual benefits that result from offering women the prospect of careers outside the "home" environment, in either the public or private sector, and those women who choose to give priority to their families also benefit from the broad background of an education when guiding their own children. But apart from this, there is ample evidence that as women increasingly attain positions of authority and influence, they contribute significantly to national policies and social development, and thus benefit society overall.

Internationalization has also contributed to the formation of different educational networks of women in the Middle East, both within their own communities and with other women all over the world. Many such networks offer varying degrees of mutual support and resources for a wide variety of beneficial initiatives aimed at improving the status of women. It is quite evident that internationalization, in all forms, is giving women in the Middle East the possibility to become global learners, and consequently to become global citizens.

An increasingly significant consequence of these developments is the fact that internationalization is making women throughout the Middle East more aware of the misconceptions that other societies have about Arab women, as well as the misconceptions that Arab women have for women in other societies. This has been a major reason behind the flourishing of different intercultural platforms that encourage communication in general, and exchanges between Arab and non-Arab women specifically. These forums are major tools that not only help correct misunderstandings, but also help both sides appreciate the cultural imperatives of women in other societies. Women's groups in the Middle East that have their roots in internationalization have influenced the decisions of local and national governments and international bodies, mostly in practical and beneficial ways.

A positive step forward would be the wide acceptance of the OECD policy brief on internationalization issues as a guideline for minimum standards, and then to further develop cooperation programs through national policies. It follows that work is needed to refine the guidelines on economic support for internationalization issues from both the private and public sectors, and that the means and responsibility for development, oversight, and guidance needs to be reviewed nationally and internationally. A high priority is for urgent development of programs to encourage more equal gender proportions of students in many disciplines.

There can be no doubt of the benefits that stem from the internationalization of education, nor of the greatly enhanced benefits of improved national and international coordination. But in order to help women in the Middle East broaden their opportunities further at an international level, internationalization policies for higher education in the region really need to be framed in terms of culture.

In light of the findings outlined in this chapter, the global communities in general and Middle Eastern states in particular need to consider the following priority areas:

- Investing in female education through internationalization. This will not only create more educational opportunities for women in the region, but will also enhance the true value of human capital. It will serve to accelerate the region's economic and social development and slow population growth, and also play a key role in alleviating poverty.

- Further research focused particularly on how internationalization can enhance the role of women in society, particularly in shaping national policies and defining the strategies to be undertaken in order to enhance women's leadership roles and women's empowerment, especially in education, science, and technology.

- Refining the guidelines on economic support for internationalization issues from both the private and public sectors, and defining how women could benefit from such support.

- Coordinating between all stakeholders to ensure a strong two-way flow for exchange programs, resulting in mutual benefits in terms of influence and understanding.

- The urgent development of cultural programs to enhance the study abroad experience is a necessary requirement to encourage equal exchanges between countries to strengthen meaningful international experiences.

- Encouraging the growth and development of female networks in the Middle East and worldwide, their solidarity, and extensive multilevel networking to make them an influential force in development, nationally and internationally.

- Efforts to improve female education through internationalization in MENA countries need to go beyond rhetoric and should involve policies and programs with measurable results. Middle Eastern governments can start by making internationalization an integral part of national development plans and monitoring progress toward those goals.

- Governments also need to make an extra effort to ensure that international education is more accessible to women, with special attention to the cultural framework and the quality of the education provided.

The spirit and aspirations associated with approaches to development that focus on women's issues, especially when these aspirations become part of a collective movement that embraces the interconnectivity of all tasks and actions, brings an influence to bear on global dynamics that transcends traditional socioeconomic development. It is an approach that places a strong emphasis on peace and prosperity. It is a known fact that women make substantial contributions to community development at many levels. The strengthening and extension of the internationalization of higher education will empower women to take their valuable abilities to the international arena for the infinitely greater benefit of present and future generations.

REFERENCES

Al-Maimouni, M. (2009, June). 64% of female college graduates unemployed. *Okaz*. Retrieved from http://www.okaz.com.sa/okaz/osf/20090601/Con20090601281506.htm

Al-Qazzat, A. (1980, October). Education for women in the Arab world. *Arab Perspectives, 1*(7).

Altbach, P. G. (2004). Globalization and the university: Myths and realities in an unequal world. *Tertiary Education and Management 10*, 3–25.

Altbach, P. G. (2005). The political economy of international higher education cooperation: Structural realities and global inequalities. Paper presented at Netherlands Organization for International Cooperation in Higher Education (Nuffic) Conference 2005, The Hague, Netherlands.

Altbach, P. G. and Knight, J. (2006). The internationalisation of higher education: Motivations and realities. In *The National Education Association (NEA) 2006 Almanac of Higher Education*. Washington, DC: National Education Association.

Arnold, D. D. (2006). [No title]. Address given to America-Mideast Educational and Training Services (AMIDEAST) at the Symposium on Egyptian Education and Training for the Global Economy, Cairo, Egypt.

Arnold, D. D. (2007). The role and reality of the university in the Middle East. Address given to the Los Angeles World Affairs Council, Los Angeles, CA.

Arnold, D. D. (2007). American universities in the Middle East: Agents for change in the Arab World. Address presented to Council on Foreign Relations, New York, NY.

Abdul Ghafour, P. K. (2007, May 27). One-third of government jobs for women: Sultan. *Arab News*. Retrieved from http://archive.arabnews.com/?page=1&section=0&article=96703&d=27&m=5&y=2007

Barwell, J. M. (2006, December). *The Texas Gulf Coast biosciences cluster: Workforce development and educational challenges*. Houston, TX: The University of Houston College of Technology, Center for Life Sciences Technology.

Brookings Institution. (2008, November). *American education in the Middle East: Smart power for a new era*. Transcript of the discussion on the future of American-style higher education in the Middle East, Washington, DC.

Deghady, S. (2008, June 18). Education reform: American style. *The Media Line, Science Development Network (SDN), Islamic Development Bank IDB.* Jeddah, Kingdom of Saudi Arabia.

Del Catillo, D. (2004, March 5). The Arab world's scientific desert. *The Chronicle of Higher Education, 50*(26).

Deloitte. (2009, April). Advancement of ME women to leadership positions: Deloitte hosts women business leaders. Retrieved March 1, 2010 from http://www.deloitte.com/view/en_QA/qa/press/press-releases/press-release/a58bcf6d88912210VgnVCM100000ba42f00aRCRD.htm

Eastwood, B. M. (2007, February). Is science the key to the Middle East? *The American, A Magazine of Ideas*.

El-Sanabary, N. (1992). *Education in the Arab Gulf states and the Arab world: An annotated bibliographic guide*. New York, NY: Garland Publishing.

Ghabra, S. & Arnold, M. (2007). Studying the American way: An assessment of American-style higher education in Arab countries. *The Washington Institute for Near East Policy, 71*(June).

Gutierrez, R., Hawthorne, A., Kirk, M., & Powers, C. (2009). *Expanding U.S. study abroad in the Arab World: Challenges and opportunities*. New York, NY: Institute of International Education.

Hamdan, A. (2005). Women and education in Saudi Arabia: Challenges and achievements. *International Education Journal, 6*(1), 42–64.

Hamrick, J. (1999). Internationalizing higher education institutions: Broadening the approach to institutional change.

Hollings Center for International Dialogue. (2007, January). *Independent universities in the Muslim World: A new approach, part II: Conference report*, Istanbul, Turkey.

Jamal, Z. (2004). *Arab human development report 2004: Towards freedom in the Arab world*. Oslo, Norway: UNDP Oslo Governance

Jaschik, S. (2005). New era in international higher education. *Inside Higher Ed*.

Kirp, D. L. (2003). *Shakespeare, Einstein, and the bottom line: The marketing of higher education*. Cambridge, MA: Harvard University Press.

Knight, J. (2003) *Internationalization of higher education practices and priorities: IAU survey report*. Paris, France: International Association of Universities.

Labi, A. (2008, July 25). World Bank urges sweeping changes in higher education across the Arab world. *The Chronicle of Higher Education, 54*(23).

Lewin, T. (2008, February 11). In oil-rich Mideast, shades of the Ivy League. *The New York Times*.

Lewin, T. (2008, April 12). Yale moves away from plans for link with Abu Dhabi. *The New York Times*.

Li & Karakowsky. (2001). Do we see eye-to-eye? Implications of cultural differences for cross-cultural management research and practice. *The Journal of Psychology, 135*(5), 501–517.

Mills, A. (2008, July 25). U.S. universities negotiate tricky terrain in the Middle East. *The Chronicle of Higher Education, 54*(46).

Sirat, M. & Kaur, S. (2007, August 31). The internationalisation of higher education: Realities and implications. *Institute Penyelidikan Pendidikan Tinggi Negara, Updates on Global Higher Education, 14*.

Nye, J. S. Jr. (2004). *Soft power: The means to success in world politics*. Cambridge, MA: PublicAffairs.

Organisation for Economic Co-operation and Development (OECD). (2004, August). *Internationalisation of higher education, policy brief, Public Affairs and Communications Directorate*. Paris, France: OECD.

Observatory on Borderless Higher Education. (2004). *Mapping borderless higher education: Policy, markets and competition*. London: Association of Commonwealth Universities.

Pollock, M. (2007, May). Qatar: A model for education reform in the Arabian Gulf. *World Education News and Reviews, 20*(5). Retrieved from http://www.wes.org

Rizvi, F. (2004). Offshore Australian higher education. *International Higher Education, 37*(fall), 7–9.

Rupp, R. (2009). Higher education in the Middle East: Opportunities and challenges for U.S. universities and Middle East partners. *Global Media Journal, 8*(14).

United Nations Development Programme. (2005). *The Arab human development report 2005: Towards the rise of women in the Arab World*. New York, NY: United Nations Publications.

World Bank. (2000). *Higher education in developing countries: Peril and promise*. Washington, DC: The World Bank.

World Bank. (2002). *The Road not travelled: Education reform in the Middle East and North Africa*. Washington, DC: The World Bank.

World Bank. (2007a). *The status & progress of women in the Middle East & North Africa*. Washington, DC: The World Bank.

World Bank. (2007b). *Middle East & North Africa: Gender overview*. Washington, DC: The World Bank.

World Bank. (2009). *The status & progress of women in the Middle East & North Africa*. Washington, DC: The World Bank.

Chapter Six

PROMOTING U.S.–MIDDLE EASTERN CULTURAL UNDERSTANDING THROUGH YOUTH EXCHANGE

SHERIFA M.B.E. FAYEZ, NATIONAL DIRECTOR, AFS EGYPT
DAN PRINZING, EDUCATION DIRECTOR, IDAHO HUMAN RIGHTS EDUCATION CENTER

> *International educational exchanges help students and educators around the world to understand one another better. Together, we must respond to the challenges of poverty and hunger, climate change, public health, and economic revitalization. . . . Through international educational exchanges, we can build bridges of respect and understanding that will connect people and enable us to work together, now and in the future, for a better world.*
>
> —United States Secretary of State Hillary Rodham Clinton, 2009

In the aftermath of September 11, 2001, Secretary of State Colin Powell stated that Americans needed to be more engaged with the rest of the world than ever before. He advocated what Charles Titus (1994) had called "a global civic culture that helps Americans recognize their obligations to their own nation and to the planet at large."

Recognizing the need to enhance international education in the schools, Fred Czarra (2002) stated that "...the study of the world can be divided into three main themes: global issues, global culture, and global connections." Each theme, integrated into instruction, promotes an engaged citizenry aware that it is residing on a planet that has become a global village—requiring what Elise Boulding (1988) has called our "...civic attention and action on a transnational and transcultural scale."

Many dedicated individuals and organizations have set out to integrate these principles into secondary education, often in the context of promoting U.S.–Middle Eastern cultural understanding. These efforts have begun both at the state level, where activists have integrated intercultural understanding into curriculum standards, as well as at the federal level, through the introduction of exchange programs for students from many states and countries. This article shows how these efforts have evolved and expanded through two case studies. The first is an examination of the Youth Exchange and Study (YES) program, which is sponsored by the U.S. Department of State and administered by AFS Egypt, and AFS-USA, AIFS Foundation, PAX, CIEE, and ACES. The second describes efforts to promote global understanding in Idaho.

The AFS Approach: Connecting Lives, Sharing Cultures

Foreseeing a basic need for communication and interaction throughout the world, AFS was established in 1947 by volunteer ambulance drivers in the First and Second World Wars who pledged to sustain their tradition of international service. The result was the creation of the AFS International Scholarships. In 1960, AFS Egypt was created to handle high school student exchange programs. Its mission is to provide intercultural learning opportunities to help people develop the knowledge, skills, and understanding needed to create a more just and peaceful world. More recently, this mission has become even more important as tensions have increased around the world, particularly between the U.S. and the Middle East. There is a genuine need for youth exchange programs that address all sectors and levels of both societies. The need for dialogue and mutual listening has become imperative.

While study abroad programs have existed in Egypt for long time, the AFS full-immersion program model, which is characterized by a homestay with an Egyptian family, is not yet instilled in Middle Eastern culture. Historically, very few well-known stories of Egyptian scholars studying abroad exist, but famous scholars like Rifa'a Al-Tahtawi (1801–1873), Imam Muhammad Abdou (1849–1905), and Taha Hussein (1889–1973) traveled to study in Europe, and each dedicated himself in his own way to reconciling cultural and intellectual differences between the West and the Islamic world. Hussein was particularly dedicated to advancing modern approaches to education, saying "knowledge is like the air we breathe and the water we drink." By sharing their uncommon and fascinating experiences in their biographies, these courageous and visionary Egyptians have inspired and encouraged generations of Egyptians to follow in their path. As postgraduate students, these scholars lived in dorms or rented apartments, along with other students from around the world—in marked contrast to today's AFS full-immersion, homestay programs for high school students.

This portion of the article discusses the AFS program in Egypt and the challenges it has faced in trying to meet the true goals of these cultural exchanges. Specifically, we look at the YES program, a case study for program approaches and challenges in youth exchanges overall.

Youth Exchange and Study (YES), a program established in October 2002 and sponsored by the U.S. Department of State, Bureau of Educational and Cultural Affairs (ECA), evolved out of a generalized recognition that public diplomacy efforts had been neglected in many countries around the world for many years. The effects of this neglect had come into stark focus in the aftermath of the events of September 11, 2001.

ECA, along with the U.S. exchange community, recognized the importance of youth exchange as a key component of a renewed commitment to building bridges between citizens of the U.S. and countries around the world, particularly those with significant Muslim populations.

The YES program provides scholarships for high school students (15–17 years old) from countries with significant Muslim populations to spend up to one academic year in the United States. Students live with host families, attend high school, engage in activities to learn about American society and values, acquire leadership skills, and help educate Americans about their countries and cultures. In 2009, the YES program was extended to offer the same opportunity to American high school students— to spend one year abroad with the same goals and aims.

In 2003, AFS Egypt agreed to work with the YES program, as partner of AFS USA. From 2003–2009, a total of 4,362 students participated in the YES program, representing Afghanistan, Albania, Bahrain, Bangladesh, Bosnia and Herzegovina, Brunei, Bulgaria, Egypt, Gaza, Ghana, Kosovo, India, Indonesia, Israel (Arab Community), Jordan, Kenya, Kuwait, Lebanon, Macedonia, Malaysia, Mali, Morocco, Mozambique, Nigeria, Oman, Pakistan, Philippines, Qatar, Saudi Arabia, Senegal, Suriname, Tanzania, Thailand, Tunisia, Turkey, West Bank, and Yemen (U.S. Department of State, 2009).

As mentioned above, hosting for an extended period of time is a highly unusual practice in the Middle East. While Middle Eastern hospitality has been famous and world-renowned throughout history, hosting a person, let alone a foreign teenager, for a whole year is rare if not unheard of. In that sense, it is only natural for families to fear and to expect the worst as their sons and daughters embark on their experience to the United States. Parents do not know what to expect of American homes and families. Often, they depend on misleading and subjective sources of information, which may include the media and the experiences of friends.

On the other hand, exchange programs and hosting students are not new to American culture and are common practice in American communities and schools. Most Americans can recall a story about an exchange student in their community from somewhere in the world, at some time during their school years. The U.S. hosted 27,924 high school exchange students in 2008/09; for every 1,250 students in Americans high schools, three are exchange students (Oliver, 2009). Over the years, experience has accumulated and acceptance of the concept has set in within the culture.

Balancing the perception of hosting on both sides of the Atlantic to help Egyptian families understand their children's experiences is an important task. The program has tried to help participating families understand the concept of welcoming, living with, and developing a relationship with a new person living in their home and among their family members. To understand hosting, participants must understand the concept of hosting a young American in an Egyptian home and hosting a young Egyptian in a home in the U.S.

With the clear goals of AFS Egypt and the YES program in mind, AFS Egypt has approached and tackled these challenges with the help of its extensive volunteer network. It is important to note that AFS Egypt is a volunteer-based organization; it is comprised of host families, host schools, alumni, and others who believe in the mission, all serving on a voluntary basis. Most volunteers are people whose lives have been touched, in some way, by an exchange experience. The following sections describe the best practices that the program has developed over the years since its inception.

Considering the YES Program as a "Family Program"

In the view of AFS Egypt, parents and siblings are just as important as the student selected on the program. They receive preparation and are involved in the program as much as possible. Efforts to integrate and involve the family begin from the very first time they hear about the program in the recruitment phase. These efforts continue throughout the selection process and preparation phases, finally ending in the reentry phase, which lasts one year after the student returns. In all, this timeline lasts at least two full years. Families are invited to fill out parts of the application, participate in interviews, attend seminars, and join workshops and orientation camps. Collectively, they are a part of their child's experience and life while abroad and during reentry.

Another important practice that has continued since the start of the YES program in Egypt is an invitation extended to the selected students and their families by the U.S. Ambassador to Egypt. The ambassador welcomes the participants and thanks their families for trusting American families to take care of their young ones. This reception marks the beginning of the experience for the students and reassures parents.

Create Communities that Understand and Support the Full-Immersion Program

Wherever AFS Egypt recruits and selects a student, the organization actively engages the family, community, and school through its local volunteers. As participants throughout the program, they have their own experiences, their own stories to tell, and a more profound and multifaceted understanding of the program. This core community of volunteers, which grows every year, normally has the following tasks:

- Recruiting and selecting the appropriate students for the program;
- Preparing and orienting students and their families for their exchange experience;
- Supporting natural families while their children are abroad;
- Supporting hosted participants and their host families;
- Working with local schools to engage in the program, either by hosting a foreign exchange student or preparing for the return of their own student after one year;
- Supporting the student upon return from his year abroad and helping him reintegrate into the community; and

- Encouraging alumni and hosted students to engage actively within their local communities.

To enhance and augment understanding of the program, regular training on intercultural learning, research outcomes, and practical program information is carried out in different chapters for volunteers all year round. Trainings address host families, counselors, schoolteachers, and chapter leaders, helping them to understand and respond to the stages of adaptation that each student experiences during his or her time abroad.

Another best practice consists of promoting two-way exchanges whenever possible. The natural family of the selected student is always encouraged to host an exchange student, in hopes that they, too, will further understand the challenges and changes that the student experiences. Thus, the student's natural family will have its own adjustment cycle and adaptation process. By hosting a student from abroad, family members are able to understand and effectively support their child both while abroad and upon return.

Promoting Intercultural Learning throughout the Program Phases

The program encourages as many students and parents as possible to attend information sessions and orientations. The goal is to expose a large group of people to intercultural learning, hosting, and the benefits of the exchange program, as well as to promote the mission of the program. Even though only 50 students can participate in the YES program each year, 200 applicant families are invited to four selection/orientation camps in the preparation phase. These orientations discuss topics like adjustment, integration, different styles of communication, stereotyping, and how to deal with difficult and ambiguous situations. Students learn about life in the U.S., schools, host families, teenage life, and, last but not least, how to appropriately represent their own country. Participants sharpen and practice their presentation and public speaking skills, enhancing their leadership ability.

Lectures for students and their families feature speakers on topics related to their experiences. Some examples of lectures include:

- The undersecretary of foreign affairs speaks to the students about public diplomacy and U.S.-Egyptian diplomatic relations.

- Older returnees, who participated in the program in the 1960s and are now prominent members of society, talk about their experiences and how their lives have developed and were shaped by their program in the U.S.

- Members of the U.S. embassy discuss and answer questions about life in the U.S.

- An Imam speaks to students about Islam in the U.S. and answers questions about living in the U.S. as a Muslim.

<u>Sharing Experiences and Stories through Meetings, Gatherings, and
Electronic Media</u>

Simple but touching stories coming from students on the program in the U.S. resonate strongly in Egypt, quickly change perceptions and misunderstandings, and give a face to the program. Families and communities listen, learn, and open their homes as they hear such stories. In return, they display unprecedented hospitality. A few example stories from Egyptian family members involved in the program follow:

- Can you believe that my son's American host mother bought him dates and *halal* meat on the first day of Ramadan to celebrate with him? When he got ill, she sat next to him and did not leave his side until he got better.

- My American host grandfather took me to the supermarket and helped me buy ingredients for an Egyptian recipe that I promised to cook for Thanksgiving. My dish turned out horrible and not at all like how it should be but my family still showed me that they enjoyed our food, and appreciated my culture. I love my host family and will never forget them.

- My whole class decided to fast one day in Ramadan with me to experience how it feels. My teacher let me talk about Ramadan to my class and we had a discussion about it afterwards. After that day, I felt that a huge barrier was removed and I made my lifetime friends.

One father from a small village in the Nile River Delta area in the north shared his story during an AFS event in Ramadan:

> When my son first applied for his exchange program in the U.S. and left, I felt that I had made a huge mistake. I knew that God would punish me for sending him to a place where Islam was frowned upon and at such a young age. But when my son arrived he found that his non-Muslim host family bought him a watch that rang five times during the day to remind him of his prayer times, they showed him the direction of the *qibla*, and took him to the nearest mosque. I felt ashamed of how I judged.

One American student wrote about her experience in Egypt:

> I feel strongly attached to the Middle East and recognize it as a significant region of the world. Before I went to Egypt, I was aware of the problems that seemed to be growing there. However, I did not concern myself with them. I felt that it was some Muslim extremist's fault for creating wars and that there was really nothing more to it. This is where my views have changed most dramatically. Whereas I laughed with my friends who told me that they hoped I would come back alive from Egypt, I now become almost appalled and angered by these kinds of jokes. It frustrates me and saddens me that the majority of American population sees the Middle East as a place only for violence, war, extreme religion and terrorism. It is true that these corrupt influences exist there. However, I had an experience most opposite from this stereotype. Though most Egyptians dislike American governmental policy, as

an American citizen, I was welcomed with open arms into the homes and hearts of more families and new friends than I can name. Bombs? I didn't see any. Members of some Islamic jihad movement that Americans panic about? I didn't meet any.

Yes, the people of Egypt are mostly Muslim, and yes, the women cover with long sleeves and veils. Yes, many stereotypes that people have about Egypt and the Middle East are partially true but in no way do these prevent the people from learning, growing and sharing. My conservative Muslim host family, who prayed five times a day, taught me only about kindness, sharing and community. My mother, who veiled from head to toe, always stayed up until I returned home safe at night. My sister, who will not date until she has accepted a marriage offer, and I bantered about the order and atomic weight of the elements on the periodic table and also which shirt looked better with which pants...

In a culture like the U.S., where hosting has existed for many years, the practice will continue to change minds and never fail to empower people to speak up. Egyptian people are touched as they hear how one Egyptian student helped his host father speak up when needed. The following letter to the editor appeared in a local newspaper in Burlington, Washington:

> Usually I don't pay much attention to opinion pieces as often the writers seem to be sadly misinformed or what I call politically infected. I was, however, awed and shocked into responding to a recent column titled "Muslim goal is to crush U.S." I was further shocked to find that no one else had complained to the [local newspaper] about this glaringly ignorant and racist headline. I am embarrassed for our community.... This unfortunate choice of words perpetuates the myth that Muslim=terrorist and paints one billion people with the same brush and falls right into the trap that the terrorists have set to divide and conquer.... This past year, I had the pleasure of hosting a Muslim student from Egypt who attended Sedro-Woolley High School. He was sponsored by the U.S. State Department in hopes of fostering a better under-standing between Arabs and Americans. I was very impressed at how well-mannered, considerate and polite he was, and I was very pleased at how well the students treated him. Apparently our young people in the community don't read our opinion pages—thank God. (Lindberg, 2005)

Such simple anecdotes that reflect the impact on both ends are exactly what youth exchange programs aim to achieve. Government statements cannot equal the testi-mony of people who have experienced, first hand, what "the other" is all about. This is among the most powerful tools we possess to thaw the ice and put a friendly face on both the American and Muslim people in the Middle East and elsewhere.

Now, eight years into the program, parents, alumni, teachers, and volunteers believe in it strongly. Egyptian families are volunteering and willing to host students in hope of making a difference and believing that they can be part of the solution. In the course of numerous exchanges between families in Egypt and in the U.S., many families have, at some point, hosted a child from the other family. This is a very powerful bond. Participants and alumni of such exchange programs refuse to accept any negative comments about their host country, be it the U.S. or Egypt—they are the strongest advocates of people-to-people relations and public diplomacy.

The YES program was evaluated by the U.S. Department of State, Bureau of Educational and Cultural Affairs, to assess the impact of the exchange experience on the YES students' attitudes and behavior over time (InterMedia Survey Institute, 2009). One strategy for determining the success of the program was to define and measure the degree to which the YES participants used their improved communication and leadership skills to share their new understanding of the United States and its people with their compatriots at home, and possibly help to break down negative stereotypes. Across all cohorts, respondents indicated that they shared information about their experiences in the United States with family, friends, and others in their communities during their first year back at home, both informally and formally.

Participants are confident that their information-sharing efforts have produced very positive results, on average and as illustrated in Table 6.1 below.

TABLE 6.1: IMPACT OF THE YES PROGRAM

Family and friends now…	Cohort 1	Cohort 2	Cohort 3	Cohort 4	Average
Understand American people better	84%	95%	93%	93%	91%
Understand the U.S. better	88%	90%	93%	93%	91%
Have a more positive opinion of American people	84%	89%	88%	88%	87%
Have a more positive opinion of the U.S.	76%	80%	87%	87%	82%

Source: InterMedia Survey Institute, 2009.

It is hoped that the hard work of many individuals to spread intercultural learning techniques, while respecting local culture, has added value and found acceptance within communities for exchange programs—even if it is one home, one family at a time.

Preparing for the World of Work—And Working in the World

Although the benefits of international education for youth are widely acknowledged, attention to global studies within K–12 education has been perceived as a luxury rather than as a necessity in most states, especially in an era of high-stakes accountability and emphasis on basic reading and writing skill development. Yet at the national level, nongovernmental organizations and corporate interests have continued to emphasize the need to put the world into world-class education. One such effort, spearheaded by the Asia Society in New York, included the development of a Community Action Kit for use in community and state policy discussion on the importance of international education and exchanges.

Drawing on the Asia Society's network, and with financial support from the Longview Foundation, Idaho launched an international education initiative in 2003. Partnering in the state's initiative, AFS Intercultural Programs has been instrumental in crafting international exchange guidelines and collaborating in the design and delivery of leadership exchange programs to directly impact teaching and learning in Idaho schools.

Idaho's 2005 revision of its K–12 content learning standards reflects an effort to internationalize coursework by including a Global Perspectives standard with learning objectives integrated into social studies courses from kindergarten through Grade 12. The state's Global Perspectives standard asserts that we "build an understanding of multiple perspectives and global interdependence" through an examination of global connections, global cultures, and global issues—an understanding that will ultimately broaden our sense of community.

Idaho's mandate for citizenship education states: "Schools will provide instruction and activities necessary for students to acquire the skills to enable them to be responsible citizens in their homes, schools, communities, state and nation." The addition of the Global Perspectives standard suggests that we need to educate U.S. citizens for responsible participation in our communities, our nation, and our interdependent world. As Titus (1994) recognized, "The future of American democracy depends in large part on how well the citizens of our nation gain the competence of citizenship needed to carry out their civic responsibilities, both here at home and in the world."

Such competence, however, cannot be fostered solely through state standards, course outlines, or textbooks. During her eight-year administration as Idaho's State Superintendent of Public Instruction (1999–2007), Dr. Marilyn Howard launched an international education initiative that included not only the revision of the state standards, but also the distribution of a policy guide for sending and receiving exchange students, the creation of over 50 lesson plans designed to bring the world into Idaho's classrooms, the partnering of sister schools around the world, and the hosting of education missions abroad for Idaho teachers and administrators. Central to the initiative was a commitment to fostering a school climate and culture that recognized the importance of supporting opportunities for students and teachers to see and experience other countries and cultures. Since 2004, Idaho educators have participated in over 15 fully grant-funded missions to the Basque Country of Spain, China, Germany, Jordan, the Republic of Korea, Mexico, the Netherlands, Poland, the Republic of Ireland, and Northern Ireland.

The Idaho initiative was reinforced by a 2006 policy statement and recommendation issued by the Washington, DC–based Committee for Economic Development:

> The cross-cultural competence that is needed to succeed in the business world may require a combination of foreign language skills, international knowledge, and international experience. Employers value meaningful international experience such as study abroad as well as the application and development of

the international skills learned in the classroom.... Foreign language skills, knowledge of other world regions and cultures, and overseas experience all contribute to create an employee who has the cross-cultural competence needed by American businesses in the twenty-first century. (p. 8)

Upon Dr. Howard's retirement from public office, the international education initiative transferred from the Idaho State Department of Education to the nonprofit Idaho Human Rights Education Center (IHREC), where she currently serves as the chair of the IHREC education committee. The IHREC is active in the Cooperative Civic Education Exchange program, and, through the Center for Civic Education in Calabasas, California, has established partnerships with the Republic of Ireland, Northern Ireland, Colombia, and Jordan to engage in the Civitas International Exchange Program.

Funded by the U.S. Department of Education under the Education for Democracy Act approved by the United States Congress, Civitas provides the means for Idaho educators and policymakers who have a direct impact on teaching and learning in Idaho's classrooms to exchange ideas and experiences in civics and government education among political, educational, governmental, and private-sector leaders in the state's partnering countries.

The IHREC requires exchange participants to observe and/or receive training in the Center for Civic Education's Project Citizen program. Project Citizen is a curricular program for middle, secondary, and postsecondary students, youth organizations, and adult groups that promotes competent and responsible participation in local and state government. The program prepares participants to monitor and influence public policy. In the process, participants develop understanding of democratic values and principles, tolerance, and feelings of political efficacy.

Participating in the 2009 IHREC Civitas mission to Jordan, Idaho state representative Brian Cronin blogged in the *Boise Weekly* that the purpose of the Middle East exchange was

> ...to discover for ourselves that much of what we know and have heard about the Arab world is steeped in misinformation. [We were] encouraged to keep our minds, ears, eyes, and hearts open...urged to ask questions and talk to Jordanians...and encouraged to take in the food, the culture, the history, and the people and enjoy a rare opportunity that most Americans will never have. (Cronin, 2009)

In one blog post, the legislator described visiting a United Nations Relief and Works Agency (UNRWA) school for Palestinian refugees in Amman:

> Once we entered, we were escorted to a 10th grade civics class. The plan was for us to see how Project Citizen truly worked in practice. The approximately 30 adolescent girls were notably more reserved in greeting us than their younger counterparts in the schoolyard.

After some brief introductions, the students began their presentations. They would speak to a series of slides that they had prepared, outlining the evolution of the Project Citizen project they had pursued over the course of several months.

I won't go into the details other than to explain that the project they chose to develop had to do with keeping the school clean and hygienic. This was the problem they had identified and settled on as being the most pressing within their school environment. As mundane as that may sound (at least it did to me), the presentation was powerful in revealing what a sweeping and transformative change the project had on school spirit, pride, and the overall learning environment. For many of the girls, who spoke to us in both Arabic and English, you got the sense that the Project Citizen had been an empowering, and even life-changing experience. They had learned a process for identifying and solving a problem—tools that they can apply to all areas of their lives. (Cronin, 2009)

For a few hours in a school, the legislator stepped into the lives of a classroom of Arab students and the exchange had accomplished its intended purpose—it had broadened an individual's perspective on the world.

The IHREC, under subcontract to AFS Intercultural Programs and funded by the U.S. Department of State, designed and delivered two leadership exchange programs that included training in Project Citizen while the participants were in Idaho. The first leadership exchange program was the 2007 Global LEAP (Leadership Exchange Abroad for Principals) program, which brought a delegation of 21 school administrators from Bolivia, Ecuador, and Venezuela to Idaho for a three-week program in local schools.

The second leadership exchange program, the 2009 Youth LEAD (Leadership, Engagement, Activism and Democratization) program, provided a mutual exchange opportunity for 36 students—18 Idaho high school students spent three weeks in Jordan and Israel and 18 students from the Middle East (six from Israel, six from Jordan, and six from Palestine) spent three weeks in Idaho. Major elements of the Idaho-based portion of this exchange program ranged from theme-based leadership development and immersion in U.S. education systems to cultural site visits and homestay residencies. Students participated in school/class shadowing of their American peers, studied the internationally recognized curriculum of Project Citizen, and interacted with the staff, board, and volunteer network associated with the Idaho Anne Frank Human Rights Memorial. Through active participation in American educational and democratic systems, as well as through one-on-one interaction with a diverse cross-section of Americans, the Middle East students gained opportunities to create sustainable ties of learning and cooperation between the United States and their home countries.

Collaborating and communicating as a virtual class, all 36 students in the program were linked through an online forum that continued throughout the year. Students completed weekly assignments, maintained a content-driven discussion board, and showcased their community action Project Citizen portfolios. Additionally, the portal served as a vehicle for capturing students' day-to-day exchange experiences and enabled students to share dozens of blog entries and hundreds of photographs.

The data gathered in the program evaluation highlight the students' recognition of the "other"—seeing the world from the perspective of another person. The students reference Middle East issues through the stories of people; they view the countries in the region as a collage of faces rather than as abstract news items.

> Before I came to Jordan quite a few of my friends said things to me like "don't get shot" and "don't become a terrorist." I am very lucky to be able to develop a new understanding of the Middle East…I know my filters are very different and I hope I will be able to bring some of my influence home.

Upon their return to the state, the students suffered from an inability to share their learning and enthusiasm with their peers. Simply put, the exchange had created a relationship with a place and its people that had changed the lives of the participants. The experience was incongruent to others' views of the world.

In his 1869 book, *The Innocents Abroad*, Mark Twain noted, "Travel is fatal to prejudice, bigotry, and narrow-mindedness, and many of our people need it solely on these accounts. Broad, wholesome, charitable views of men and things cannot be acquired by vegetating in one little corner of the earth all one's lifetime." What the Idaho students had witnessed abroad had new meaning when they returned home and took a new look at their own communities. They were eager to share cultural connections when the students from the Middle East arrived in Boise; connections that included the oldest synagogue west of the Mississippi and an Islamic Center with members representing over 45 different countries.

The Idaho Human Rights Education Center, with an infrastructure and institutional base developed to support youth and adult exchange, is committed to bringing the world to its geographically large, population-sparse corner of the earth. The impact of the Middle East exchanges have rippled through the participants' plans for the future, and reached into their schools and communities. Notably, several of the Idaho Youth LEAD students have recommended policy changes to enhance international education and community service in their school districts as their culminating Project Citizen projects.

Speaking before an audience of 200 IHREC supporters in fall 2009, Hannah Schwarz, one Idaho Youth LEAD student, stated:

> Our trip consisted of three parts: Jordan, Israel, and Washington, DC, which yielded three very different experiences and feelings. Jordan was about beauty. We were enchanted by the beautiful landscape throughout the coun-

try. Jordan was about hospitality. Never in my life have I felt more welcomed and at home. Jordan was about love—about a group of 18 kids from Idaho completely falling in love with a country and its people. While we were in Jordan, we lived in complete bliss. We experienced a new culture that had undeniable beauty, and, for most, crossing over the Allenby Bridge into Israel was bittersweet, but our time in Israel was invaluable: it opened our eyes to the harsh reality of living in an area of conflict.

Being in Israel was emotionally draining, but an experience I will carry with me for the rest of my life. Israel was about reality, about witnessing the valid points of both sides. Since the trip I have learned that understanding and cultural awareness lays the foundation for open communication, the first step towards peace. Taking part in the Youth LEAD program showed me an entirely new world. Each person we met had a unique story, but overall, everyone had the same dream of a future of peace.

With an organizational mission to promote respect for human dignity and diversity through education, the IHREC asserts that classroom discussion and investigation of the world is an imperative. By drawing upon "…the cross-cultural experiences of students and teachers who have studied/taught abroad, participated in various international activities, [or] engaged in international travel…teachers can open a door to a work of experiences that address a variety of interests, beliefs, and practices of other cultures" (Taylor, 1996).

Conclusion

While Idaho's original goal might have been to bring the world into its classrooms, the hallmark of the initiative has been its commitment to get teachers and students out into the world. That accomplishment alone has fostered a global perspective that reaches into classrooms—and communities—throughout the state. The success of the initiative also testifies to the success of building partnerships at the state, national, and international levels. Schools in Idaho rely upon established programs to facilitate the sending and hosting of high school students; AFS Intercultural Programs relies upon the schools' capacity to institutionalize international exchange.

The case studies highlight the value-added impact that exchange brings to K–12 education; impact that is captured in the global issues, global culture, and global connections that the participants witness. As President Obama so eloquently said while visiting Cairo in June 2009:

> So long as our relationship is defined by our differences, we will empower those who sow hatred rather than peace, those who promote conflict rather than the cooperation that can help all of our people achieve justice and prosperity. And this cycle of suspicion and discord must end…. On education, we will expand exchange programs and increase scholarships like the one that brought my father to America. (Obama, 2009)

REFERENCES

Boulding, E. (1988). *Building a global civic culture: Education for an interdependent world*. New York, NY: Teachers College Press.

Committee for Economic Development. (2006). *Education for global leadership: The importance of international studies and foreign language education for U.S. economic and national security*. Washington, DC: Committee for Economic Development.

Cronin, B. (2009, December 3). Jordan late-blogging: A school, a camel and the King [Web log message]. Retrieved March 12, 2010 from http://www.boiseweekly.com/TheGrip/archives/2009/12/03/jordan-late-blogging-a-school-a-camel-and-the-king

Czarra, F. (2002). Global education checklist for teachers, schools, school systems and state education agencies. *Issues in Global Education, 173*. New York, NY: American Forum for Global Education.

InterMedia Survey Institute (Ed.). (2009). Evaluation of the youth exchange and study program. Washington, DC: U.S. Department of State, Bureau of Educational and Cultural Affairs.

Lindberg, B. (2005, December). Shock and awe for ignorance about Muslims. [Letter to the editor]. *The Argus*.

Obama, B. (2009, June 4). The President's speech in Cairo: A new beginning. Retrieved February 25, 2010 from http://www.whitehouse.gov/blog/NewBeginning/

Oliver, E. (Ed.). (2009). *International youth exchange statistics*. Alexandria, VA: CSIET: Council on Standards for International Educational Travel.

Rules of the Board Governing Education (Idaho). (2009). 08.02.03.170 Citizenship. Retrieved March 12, 2010 from http://adm.idaho.gov/adminrules/rules/idapa08/0203.pdf

Schwarz, H. (2009, September 25). *Youth LEAD presentation*. Presented at the Idaho Human Rights Education Center "Change Your World Celebration," Boise, Idaho.

Taylor, H. E. (1996). *Practical suggestions for teaching global education*. Washington, DC: Educational Resources Information Center.

Titus, C. (1994). Civic education for global understanding. Washington, DC: Educational Resources Information Center.

U.S. Department of State, Bureau of Educational and Cultural Affairs. (2009). Youth exchange and study program (YES). Retrieved February 25, 2010 from http://exchanges.state.gov/youth/programs/yes.html

Chapter Seven

ADVANCING U.S. STUDY ABROAD
IN THE ARAB WORLD

JEROME B. BOOKIN-WEINER, DIRECTOR OF STUDY ABROAD, AMIDEAST
AHMAD Y. MAJDOUBEH, DEAN OF THE FACULTY OF FOREIGN LANGUAGES,
  UNIVERSITY OF JORDAN[1]

Historical Overview of Study Abroad to the Middle East

American students have always been present on Arab and Middle Eastern campuses, not only at American-style colleges, such as the American University of Beirut and the American University in Cairo, but also at mainstream Arab universities, such as Cairo University in Egypt, Damascus University in Syria, and the University of Jordan in Amman. American interest in the Middle East dates back before the times of Washington Irving, Ralph Waldo Emerson, Herman Melville, and Mark Twain, all of whom visited and/or wrote about the region. Even earlier, Jonathan Edwards and the Puritans also wrote about Islam and the Arab East.

Modern educational exchange between the U.S. and the Arab world has a relatively short history. The earliest formal program in the Arab Middle East was the Center for Arabic Study Abroad (CASA), established in 1967 by a consortium of U.S. universities to offer intensive Arabic language training at the American University in Cairo. In its more than 40 years of operation, CASA has trained more than 1,350 students. Throughout its existence, CASA has received significant funding support from the U.S. Department of Education.

Also in the 1960s, the Experiment in International Living (now known as World Learning and operating study abroad programs as SIT Abroad) facilitated student enrollment in universities in Tunisia and Morocco, but those programs were not sustained. SIT Abroad began its current program in Morocco in 1988, its first in the Arab world. Today SIT Abroad also operates programs in Jordan, Tunisia, and Oman. Beginning in 1971, there were additional summer Arabic language programs in Morocco (for one year) and in Tunisia (for several years) sponsored by the University of Texas and University of Utah, respectively, and funded by the U.S. Department of Education. Those too were not sustained when the federal support was withdrawn.

Some well-known individuals, such as General John Abizaid, former Commander of the U.S. Central Command, studied Arabic at the University of Jordan in the early 1980s. In 1984, the University of Virginia started a summer Arabic program at Yarmouk University that continues today, and several religious, military, diplomatic, and other organizations and education providers sent handfuls of students to the region for varying periods of stay in the 1980s and 1990s.

However, the presence of such students has been at best marginal and sporadic, and tied primarily to studying colloquial and/or Modern Standard Arabic. The available numbers suggest that up until the end of the 20th century, the Arab world was not a particularly attractive destination for American students. The Persian Gulf War heightened interest in the region, leading to slowly mounting numbers in the 1990s.

U.S. study abroad programs in the Arab world have already expanded significantly in the early years of the present century. This is not primarily the result of conscious efforts by stakeholders in the programs. Rather, developments and events leading to heightened American consciousness of the region have been the primary factor, and globalization in general and its impact on student interests have played a secondary role. Two crucial questions, however, need to be addressed: the first is how to make these programs fulfilling and rewarding to participants and providers, and the second is how to sustain interest and enrollment in these programs beyond the spike in interest caused by the present political or historic moment. To answer these two questions, we need to briefly address a host of related issues: why American students opt to study in the Arab world, how many are coming now and in what fashion or form, the types of programs they join, the major constraints affecting these programs, and some of the main ways of enhancing the effectiveness and sustainability of these programs. All these questions must be considered in any effort to advance U.S. study abroad to the Arab world.

The Numbers

The best source of data on the flow of students from the U.S. to the Arab world for academic credit is *Open Doors: Report on International Educational Exchange*, issued annually by the Institute of International Education. The following table contains IIE's data from 1999/2000 to the present,[2] broken down by destination country (data for Cyprus, Israel, and Turkey are also included in this chart for comparison purposes):

Chapter Seven | Jerome B. Bookin-Weiner, Ahmad Y. Majdoubeh
ADVANCING U.S. STUDY ABROAD IN THE ARAB WORLD

Country	1999/00	2000/01	2001/02	2002/03	2003/04	2004/05	2005/06	2006/07	2007/08
Algeria	0	0	0	0	0	0	1	0	0
Bahrain	0	2	3	0	3	3	1	33	37
Egypt	388	436	241	303	573	807	983	1,100	1,466
Iran	0	1	2	1	1	1	0	2	1
Jordan	86	83	37	29	65	171	309	231	486
Kuwait	2	3	4	6	3	2	1	2	35
Lebanon	13	19	16	14	23	43	46	14	31
Libya	0	0	0	0	0	0	0	0	2
Mauritania	1	2	1	4	3	0	1	0	14
Morocco	132	245	170	191	298	339	370	491	719
Oman	0	0	1	0	1	2	23	21	33
Palestinian Territories	1	1	0	0	1	23	25	7	4
Qatar	0	0	0	0	2	7	2	2	24
Saudi Arabia	2	1	1	2	2	1	1	3	2
Sudan	0	0	0	0	0	1	43	4	2
Syria	5	3	2	4	19	19	39	21	22
Tunisia	59	69	20	0	11	29	54	63	173
United Arab Emirates	5	5	7	12	20	84	146	173	345
Western Sahara	0	1	0	0	0	0	0	0	0
Yemen	1	3	0	1	7	2	4	24	20
Arab World Total	**695**	**874**	**505**	**567**	**1,032**	**1,534**	**2,049**	**2,191**	**3,416**
Cyprus	15	37	77	10	38	129	125	192	203
Israel	3,898	1,248	1,031	340	665	1,617	1,981	2,226	2,322
Turkey	99	234	129	228	200	454	694	924	1,172
Other Total	**4,012**	**1,519**	**1,237**	**578**	**903**	**2,200**	**2,800**	**3,342**	**3,697**

Source: Bhandari, R. & Chow, P. (2009). *Open doors 2009: Report on international educational exchange.* New York: Institute of International Education.

These data demonstrate that Egypt and Morocco have been the regional leaders in the past decade, with Jordan and more recently the United Arab Emirates also receiving significant numbers. Events in the region have a clear impact. In the Arab world the numbers were mounting prior to September 11 and then declined for two years before rebounding dramatically, to the point that the total number of American study abroad students in Arab countries in 2007/08 (the last year for which data are available) is nearly five times the number in 1999/2000 and nearly seven times the number in 2001/02. The rebound after the initial effects of September 11 has been very rapid, with large leaps in every year except 2006/07.

Events in the region also have a clear impact on study abroad in individual countries. For example, the number of students going to Lebanon mounted steadily from 2002/03 through 2005/06, but during the summer of 2006 an armed conflict broke out between the Israeli military and Hezbollah forces in Lebanon. International students in Lebanon for summer Arabic programs had to be evacuated and the number of students consequently declined the following year. Two years later, student numbers had reached only three-fourths of the total prior to the conflict. As a point of comparison, the impact of the second Intifada and related events can be seen in the rapid decline in students going to Israel. From 1999/2000 to 2002/03, the number of students declined by over 90 percent, and at this time have not reached 1999/2000 levels.

Unfortunately, IIE's data do not include length of stay by country (i.e., did a student enroll for an academic year, semester, summer, or short-term program). However, over the same period in the world as a whole more and more students have opted for short-term programs of various lengths—some of them as short as three days, others as long as 10 weeks.

Most students studying abroad in the United Arab Emirates are likely attending short-term programs: Dubai, for example, has been a destination for many MBA students arriving for short visits. On the other hand, Egypt, Morocco, and Jordan all have a mix of semester and academic-year students as well as students in the country for shorter programs.

Why American Students Want to Study in the Arab World

Study of Arabic is the single most important driver of study abroad in the Arab world, and the rapid increase in the number of students in Arabic language courses over the past decade has driven a significant increase in study abroad numbers as well. Historically, from World War II until the 1990s, most American students in the Arab world were graduate students in Arabic, Middle East, and Islamic studies. They went to the region, overwhelmingly, to improve their language skills in preparation for undertaking research. Those undergraduates who did venture into the region had very few options open to them. The American University in Cairo and its Arabic Language Institute was the primary destination. Others included the Arabic for Speakers of Other Languages Program at the University of Jordan (in operation since the early 1980s), the School for International Training's program in Rabat, Morocco (begun in 1988), and the summer programs at AUC, the Bourguiba School in Tunis, and Yarmouk University in Irbid, Jordan (the program run by the University of Virginia). The Center for Arabic Study Abroad (CASA) program in Cairo began in 1967, with support from the U.S. Department of Education, and quickly became the standard by which all programs are judged (a role it maintains today, more than 40 years later). Throughout this period, most students enrolled primarily to improve Arabic skills in preparation for scholarly research or for careers in the State Department and other government agencies and nongovernmental organizations. Other students of Arab ancestry were interested in studying in Arab countries, often for more personal reasons.

As already noted, this situation began to shift in the 1990s, with a rapid acceleration after September 11. The Persian Gulf War led to a rise in interest in the region, and more and more institutions began to offer Arabic and courses on the region. In 2007 the Modern Language Association published statistics on the growth of Arabic language enrollments from its 2006 survey of language enrollments:

TABLE 7.2: FALL 2002 AND 2006 LANGUAGE COURSE ENROLLMENTS IN U.S. INSTITUTIONS OF HIGHER EDUCATION (IN DESCENDING ORDER OF 2006 TOTALS)

Language	2002	2006	% Change
Spanish	746,267	822,985	10.3
French	201,979	206,426	2.2
German	91,100	94,264	3.5
American Sign	60,781	78,829	29.7
Italian	63,899	78,368	22.6
Japanese	52,238	66,605	27.5
Chinese	34,153	51,582	51
Latin	29,841	32,191	7.9
Russian	23,921	24,845	3.9
Arabic	10,584	23,974	126.5
Greek, Ancient	20,376	22,849	12.1
Hebrew, Biblical	14,183	14,140	-0.3
Portuguese	8,385	10,267	22.4
Hebrew, Modern	8,619	9,612	11.5
Korean	5,211	7,145	37.1
Other languages	25,716	33,728	31.2
Total	1,397,253	1,577,810	12.9

Source: Furman, N., Goldberg, D., & Lusin, N. (2007, November). *Enrollments in languages other than English in United States institutions of higher education, fall 2006.* New York, NY: Modern Language Association. Retrieved from http://www.mla.org/2006_flenrollmentsurvey

TABLE 7.3: ARABIC ENROLLMENTS AT U.S. INSTITUTIONS OF HIGHER EDUCATION, 1980–2006

1980	3,387
1986	3,417
1990	3,475
1995	4,444
1998	5,505
2002	10,584
2006	23,974

Source: Furman, Goldberg, & Lusin, 2007.

When the MLA releases its next set of statistics in 2010 (the survey was conducted in fall 2009), we expect to see another significant increase in Arabic language enrollments. Anecdotal evidence suggests that the pace has slowed somewhat—not surprising given the extremely rapid rise from 2002–2006 and the new, higher baseline figure. The number of institutions offering Arabic is also expected to show another marked increase, as are persistence rates from first-year to second-year courses.

Traditionally, three distinct groups of American students went to the Arab world—heritage learners, those preparing for scholarly careers in Middle East and North African studies, and those interested in other careers in the region or related to the region (prospective diplomats, analysts, development professionals, and those committed to political causes related to regional affairs). However, in the past decade we have observed the emergence of three distinct new groups. The largest is composed of international studies majors who have a special interest in the region but who do not necessarily intend to pursue careers related to the region. Another significant group is composed of students who find the region interesting but who have no special interest or desire to continue studying the language or the culture after their time abroad. Some members of this group are international studies majors. Finally, there is a group of students motivated by the events of September 11 who either are seeking to contextualize the events, or who wish to become actively involved in efforts to counter "Islamic radicalism" in various ways.

Why Institutions in the Region Welcome American Students

Nearly all Arab universities and institutions of higher learning, including those in countries that are at odds with the U.S. politically, welcome American students on their campuses, almost without any reservations or second thoughts. Higher education institutions in the U.S. enjoy a worldwide reputation and prestige, and students from American campuses are therefore perceived as a positive addition to Arab campuses. We should hasten to add, however, that the number of international students on Arab university campuses is growing significantly as part of the increase in international mobility of higher education students worldwide. While most students come from other Arab countries, significant numbers come from other Muslim countries as well as from Africa, Asia, Europe, and the United States.

In our experience, Arab institutions want to host and admit American college students for two specific reasons. First, Arab universities generally are committed to facilitating and supporting the learning and understanding of the Arabic language, Islam, and Arab culture. In this context it is important to note that nearly all Arab universities, or the ministries of higher education under whose auspices they function, consider the national and international promotion and support of the Arabic language part and parcel of their mission. The second reason is the link between the Arabic language and Arab identity—a link that is deeply felt throughout the Arab world, both among academics and the general public. Many Arabs are somewhat disappointed that, at the university level, a number of disciplines (medicine, engineering, and other sciences) are taught in English, or in some places French, instead of Arabic, despite legal stipulations that Arabic should be the official language of instruction. As a consequence, English and French are seen by some as rival languages. Some view Arabic language programs on Arab campuses as a way to counter the "hegemony" of English or French and validate the learning of Arabic as an international language.

Just as Americans after September 11 felt the need to better understand Islam and the Arab world, many Arabs felt—with just as much a sense of necessity and urgency—the need to be understood by America and other Western countries. For decades, Arabs have felt a compelling need to explain themselves, in relation to a host of fundamental issues including the question of Palestine, the Arab-Israeli conflict, the role of women, and the image and message of Islam. This need is particularly strong vis-à-vis the Western world, and primarily the United States. The arrival of more American students and academics provides Arab institutions (so the thinking goes) with opportunities for the kinds of person-to-person encounters that will make understanding possible. A small but growing number of academics see the arrival of American students as a double gain: a chance for them to understand Islam and Arab culture, and also to help Arab students of English and American literature understand American culture better.

There is a second significant way in which the presence of American students contributes directly to a major mission objective of Arab universities: internationalization. For most of the 20th century, Arab universities thought of themselves as national or regional universities, but when globalization took hold and when university rankings started to crop up, Arab universities began to feel a real pressure to internationalize, especially since none of them made it into the initial lists of the world's top 500 universities. American students, who come in larger numbers than any others from outside the region, are seen as directly contributing to Arab universities' international activity, and as essential components of a diversified, multicultural, international campus.

Types of Programs That Have Emerged

Several different program models have emerged to accommodate the growing number of U.S. students interested in the region. These include:

- Traditional semester and academic-year programs operated by institutions in the region (such as the American University in Cairo, American University in Beirut, American University in Sharjah, and Al Akhawayn University in Ifrane, Morocco).

- Traditional one-for-one student exchanges with institutions in the region (almost exclusively with institutions modeled on the American system delivering courses in English).

- "Island programs" operated by third-party providers such as the School for International Training (in Morocco, Jordan, Oman, and Tunisia),

International Studies Abroad (in Morocco), IES (in Morocco), CIEE (in Morocco), and AMIDEAST (in Morocco, Egypt, and Jordan).

- Hybrid programs (programs combining elements of an island program and some integration on a local university campus) operated by third-party providers such as AMIDEAST (in Kuwait and Egypt), Middlebury (in Egypt), and CIEE (in Jordan).

- Summer language programs, which are proliferating throughout the region and are now available through local universities and language academies in a number of countries. Some are also operated by third-party providers such as SIT, CIEE, ISA, IES, and AMIDEAST.

- Short-term programs come in a number of varieties, ranging in length from a few days to several weeks. Many are groups put together by a faculty member from one institution who travels, usually to only one country but occasionally to more than one, with the students on a program that may take place during January, over spring break, or in the summer. Some of these programs are managed entirely by the institution and the faculty member. Others avail themselves of the services of a provider organization to assist with everything from arranging and managing the entire program to providing a venue for lectures. Sometimes the local provider is a university, and sometimes an American organization with a local presence, such as AMIDEAST.

Challenges and Constraints

The overall results of most U.S. study abroad programs in the Arab world are generally satisfactory to the stakeholders concerned (the students themselves, their parents, the faculty members, the sending institutions, the host institutions, the education providers, etc.). Strengths and successes can certainly be found in most of these programs (as analyses of evaluation reports by the various stakeholders reveal). Nevertheless, significant challenges and constraints still exist, both in the Arab world and in the U.S. for those interested in advancing study abroad in the region.

It has to be remembered, at the outset, that even though foreign students (including American students) have been coming to universities in the region for decades to study Arabic, area-studies courses (i.e., courses tailored to be taught in English about themes and subjects pertaining to the region) are a fairly recent development. The rapid growth of student numbers, courses offered, and study abroad programs is also a recent phenomenon. Not surprisingly, most programs offered to incoming groups of American students are new, and face the challenges and constraints typical of any new program.

As many in the field of education abroad have noted, students who are desirous of joining these programs are often unable to do so, either because of the programs' affordability and related issues of equity and access, or because of perceptions about the region. Other challenges may arise from students' expectations and backgrounds, how education providers manage the programs, faculty preparedness, course offerings and course content, and the level of readiness of the host institutions.

The intention here is not to be exhaustive in dealing with the challenges and constraints, but to address the three most prominent, salient, and all-encompassing of them: perceptions of the region, the host institutions' *preparedness* to receive students, and the sending institutions' *commitment* to send students on the program.

Perceptions of the Region

American stereotypes about the Arab and Muslim worlds have deep roots, going back to the 16th and 17th centuries when the Christian and Muslim worlds confronted each other in epic fashion at the gates of Vienna. This is not the place to retrace that history, but simply to acknowledge that it exists and continues to color perceptions in subtle yet real ways. Media portrayals of current events in the region exacerbate this fact. The turmoil surrounding the two Gulf wars, the violence of the Palestinian-Israeli conflict, civil wars in places like Lebanon and Yemen, and the ongoing violence in Algeria all lead many students (and more importantly their parents) to conclude that the Arab world is not a safe place to study. We know this is not the case, but the perception is real and has a major impact.

U.S. Department of State travel alerts and travel warnings heighten concern about certain countries. A significant number of institutions place major obstacles in front of students wanting to study in places like Lebanon, Yemen, and Israel as a result of these travel warnings.

Host Institution Preparedness

Institutions in the Arab world, as noted earlier, are eager to receive students. They are also willing, often slowly and over time, to learn how to satisfy the demands of students and providers. However, readiness is as important as willingness, and here there are a number of obvious constraints. One has to do with available infrastructure, which is often not up to expectations, as many of the host institutions in the region are public institutions with limited budgets and large student populations to serve. As a consequence, they struggle to achieve their primary missions, thus limiting their ability to meet the needs of other groups. Another constraint is the somewhat rigid bureaucracy that affects the handling of fiscal affairs, registration, and logistical matters, which can often cause delays in decisions pertaining to key questions that effective programs for international students must address.

More important than these are challenges related to the academic dimension of the programs: orientation, syllabi, and teaching. Orientation is crucial. Often, American students come with expectations unknown to the host institution, and some even expect that things at the host institution will be (and should be) exactly like at their home institution. When deconstructing this assumption through an orientation program, it is important to recognize that immense cultural barriers exist, both in the society at large and in the academic cultures of universities in the U.S. and in the Arab world. A good orientation should be a collaborative effort between the host and the provider, and should play a key role in preparing students to make the most out of their learning experiences on campus and in the community at large.

Another academic challenge has to do with syllabi. American students are used to detailed syllabi that spell out all matters pertaining to the courses they study in the clearest terms possible, including very specific information about weekly readings, exams, term papers, and presentations. While some academics in the Middle East are reasonably familiar with what a U.S. syllabus includes, most are not. They come from a tradition where either there are no syllabi handed to students in courses at all or where the syllabi are general and brief. Therefore, all those involved in these programs (especially professors) need to be made fully aware of student expectations, and often a representative of the provider needs to coordinate with the host institution closely to produce such syllabi. Providers, whether in the region or in the U.S., need to be aware of student expectations and proactive about helping to adjust them when necessary.

A bigger academic challenge is class management. Generally, American students come from a tradition where the subject material is questioned and discussed, and where class meetings allow ample opportunity to express opinions and challenge assumptions. What we are talking about here, in a sense, is student-centered learning. Most professors in the region, on the other hand, come from a tradition in which classes are large and teacher-centered, and in which students are either polite receivers of information or deferential knowledge seekers. This applies, to a great extent, to the teaching and learning of Arabic, but also to area studies classes, most of which are in the humanities and social sciences—disciplines that are greatly affected by local traditions of teaching and learning. Some discomfort and tension can occur in classes if these different traditions are not explained fully to students, professors, and administrators, and if they are not addressed by all concerned.

Sending Institution Commitment

While host institution preparedness is a huge responsibility and challenge, the commitment of the sending institution is also important. Sustainability is crucial for study abroad programs in the region. Their quality and fate depend on how many students enroll in them over the long term. While some educational institutions (as in the world of business) find themselves coping well with and willing to adapt to rapidly shifting "market" demands, most of them, we would like to suggest, do a better job introducing, developing, and managing long-term programs that meet a stable and constant demand. Actions and reactions in the world of academia are, traditionally, slower than in the world of business.

Commitment to long-term program sustainability entails obtaining local knowledge in order to understand which partners are appropriate and able to deliver the kind of programming the sending institution or organization desires for its students. As in many other regions, in the Arab world building relationships takes time and a regular presence, particularly as a program is being designed and initiated. Because of some of the challenges noted above, the combination of local knowledge and developing relationships is even more important in the Arab world than in many other places. This requires that institutions and organizations interested in providing programs in the region spend time there, get to know their counterparts (often through multiple visits over many months or years) and get to know the issues and constraints their counterparts face navigating the local academic, legal, and cultural milieu. It also means, as mentioned above, that student expectations must be managed through detailed pre-departure communications.

The Road Ahead

Sustainability, as noted above, is crucial for study abroad programs. Many at the host institutions have wondered how long this spike in interest in the Arab world will continue. Those asking the question realize that if these programs are to be effective and successful, the host institutions will have to devote considerable attention and resources to them: building adequate infrastructure, hiring administrative and academic personnel, training these personnel, changing some regulations and laws, and modifying procedures and traditions in order to cater better to these students, to name a few. All of these require a degree of assurance about the durability of the programs. Suspensions of programs during periods of conflict, even for no more than a semester, have made some top administrators at the region's universities rethink the wisdom of investing so much in these programs. Sustainability really is crucial, and much of the welfare of such programs depends at the end of the day on how many students enroll.

If one assumes, as we do, that circumstances in the region will generally be stable and favorable and that American interest in the Middle East will not fade with the changing international climate, then sustainability of the programs will depend on their quality. This is why, if these programs are to endure, all those involved need to endeavor to deliver what they promise, and to convince students and (primarily) their parents of the value and relevance of these programs. To this end, host institutions in the region need to centralize these programs on their campuses as much as possible. Until now, most programs have been somewhat marginal, existing as special programs in peripheral units.

While we believe that these programs should be diverse, catering to all program lengths, host institutions should consider allowing Americans and other international students to enroll in some of the courses in their core curricula and disciplines. So far, most courses taken by American students are tailored courses—especially designed for them and taken only by them. While tailored courses should continue to exist to meet specific needs and requests, other core courses—including, within the same core lecture halls, students from the Middle East, America, and other regions—should be revised to make it possible for study abroad students to join them. This is the best solution to the challenge of sustainability.

The fact that American students are coming to Middle Eastern institutions via study abroad programs in significant numbers is almost a miracle; it will take another miracle to sustain these programs and enable them to truly succeed, a miracle based not so much on willingness to send or receive students, but full readiness to do so.

Expanding U.S. Study Abroad in the Arab World—An IIE Workshop and White Paper

In March 2008, the Hollings Center for International Dialogue and IIE convened a workshop at Al Akhawayn University in Ifrane, Morocco to explore the challenges and opportunities in expanding American study abroad in the Arab world. The purpose of the workshop was to examine the issues that will arise as more U.S. students seek to study in the region. The Hollings Center and IIE invited 33 senior-level administrators and faculty from higher education institutions based in the U.S. and the Arab world, program provider organizations, and Arabic language centers. Participants represented 11 Arab countries and the United States.

The workshop resulted in a definition of issues and strategies that will lead to positive study abroad experiences for students in the region. At the institutional level, administrators of both sides must address issues of credit transfer and academic standards, maintaining quality while ensuring effective cultural learning experiences. Both sides must understand that resource limitations, more than limitations of will, may temper enthusiasm for growth, forcing both sides to work in creative ways to overcome barriers. At the student level, educators in the United States and the Arab world must ensure that students properly understand the challenges involved in studying in this region. Educators must develop a comprehensive knowledge of the unique cultural, historical, and linguistic context that each study abroad opportunity in the region provides, and advise students accordingly.

The workshop also led to the publication of an IIE white paper, "Expanding U.S. Study Abroad in the Arab World." For the full text, visit www.iie.org/en/Research-and-Publications.

---

[1] This chapter primarily addresses the Arab world. It excludes Turkey and Israel, which are also key destinations for American students in the region more broadly defined. It should be noted that the numbers in those two countries are roughly equal to the total in the rest of the Arab world on an annual basis, but the profile of students going to each of these countries is very different. Our impression is that in Israel the vast majority are Jewish Americans who choose to study there for cultural or religious reasons, while in Turkey the overwhelming majority participate in short-term programs, to a degree far exceeding the overall rate of short-term program participation worldwide.

[2] *Open Doors* data is available at http://opendoors.iienetwork.org

Chapter Eight

THE U.S. ARABIC DISTANCE LEARNING NETWORK: AN EFFORT TO EXPAND INSTRUCTION IN A LESS COMMONLY TAUGHT LANGUAGE

NORMAN J. PETERSON, VICE PROVOST FOR INTERNATIONAL EDUCATION,
   MONTANA STATE UNIVERSITY
YVONNE M. RUDMAN, DIRECTOR FOR ACADEMIC AND TECHNICAL PROGRAMS IN
   THE OFFICE OF INTERNATIONAL PROGRAMS, MONTANA STATE UNIVERSITY

Current global trends pose unprecedented challenges to foreign language programs in U.S. higher education institutions. These challenges are most vividly exemplified by the urgent need to expand Arabic language programs in light of the global challenges that have emerged since 9/11. This has been widely expressed in such programs as the National Security Language Initiative, the National Security Education Program's Language Flagship, and many others. Institutions have developed creative solutions to expanding Arabic language education, and according to one Modern Language Association study, Arabic enrollments in U.S. colleges and universities increased 127 percent from 2002 to 2006. One innovative approach to expanding access to Arabic is the U.S. Arabic Distance Learning Network (USADLN) initiated by Montana State University, with funding from the National Security Education Program (NSEP) and the Fund for the Improvement of Postsecondary Education (FIPSE). This essay examines this initiative as a promising and affordable approach to providing quality instruction in Arabic, and potentially in other languages, to students across the fabric of U.S. higher education.

New Challenges to Foreign Language Education

U.S. foreign language education in the first decade of the 21st century is caught between opposing global forces with radically different and often conflicting implications. On the one hand, globalization and the widespread use of English in the global marketplace cause many students and education leaders to question the need to know other languages. This interpretation is reflected in lower enrollments in foreign language courses and declining budgets for language departments, ultimately resulting in the elimination of some languages at hard-pressed colleges and universities, especially as the recession has taken its toll on higher education budgets. On the other hand, globalization is also pulling language programs at U.S. universities and colleges away from their traditional Eurocentrism. This is exemplified in the economic and political rise of Asia and the concomitant need to offer Hindi, Japanese, and Mandarin Chinese, as well as other languages such as Korean and Thai.

In the case of Arabic, these trends are even clearer. The events of 9/11 constituted the mother of all wake-up calls to the inadequacy of U.S. language education. In the aftermath of the attacks, our lack of Arabic language skills became a serious national security issue. In addition to our need for Arabic language speakers to meet the specific needs of the law enforcement, defense, and intelligence communities, it became abundantly clear that we also needed Arabic language speakers to help bridge the huge cultural gap between the U.S. and the Arabic-speaking world.

Thus, as budget pressures and the global use of English are pushing us to offer fewer languages, countervailing pressures are pulling us to expand language offerings well beyond the traditional group of European languages offered on most college and university campuses. This is the quandary facing U.S. higher education institutions as they strive to preserve their foreign language programs and stretch to offer additional critical languages.

The Dilemma: Quality vs. Affordability

The usual instructional options available to language departments are not well suited to deal with this situation. The ideal traditional approach to providing foreign language instruction, creating a faculty line for a tenure track professor, offers the probability of excellent instruction, but at a very high price. The salary for a new assistant foreign language professor averages more than $50,000 per year according to the 2009–10 *Almanac of Higher Education*, an assortment of key data published by the *Chronicle of Higher Education*. Add a benefit package, a modest allotment for professional development, and a few other incidentals and the cost quickly closes in on $100,000. In addition, for many languages, such as Arabic, there is a major shortage of qualified faculty, so even if an institution can afford a full faculty line, it is a challenge to find a qualified person to fill it.

The alternative option frequently adopted to offer less commonly taught languages, hiring a native speaker as an adjunct instructor, usually is a much more affordable approach, but the savings often come at the cost of lower-quality instruction. Just being able to speak a language does not mean you can teach it, as thousands of struggling students in language classes taught by uncredentialed native speakers will attest. This is not to say that no native-speaking adjunct faculty provide quality instruction; many do. What is clear, in any case, is that this is not an approach that offers consistent and high-quality language instruction.

So institutions are caught in a dilemma, with unaffordability on the one hand and mediocrity on the other. If U.S. colleges and universities are going to make substantial progress in providing instruction in Arabic and other needed, less commonly taught languages, this dilemma must be overcome.

The U.S. Arabic Distance Learning Network Model

The U.S. Arabic Distance Learning Network (USADLN) was developed by Montana State University to offer an alternative to these options that provides both quality and affordability. It began with this question—if institutions like Montana State cannot afford to invest in a full-time professor of Arabic, is it possible to configure a set of affordable resources that can provide a high-quality Arabic program? In response, a strategy began to take shape centering around four learning elements—remotely located faculty expertise, new technologies, native-speaking international students, and study abroad.

The Network, as its name implies, utilizes emerging distance education technologies as a key element in its design. Through interactive video facilities linked through broadband Internet connections, the Network brings instruction from a highly qualified professor of Arabic to students at participating institutions across the country. In this way, the Network not only makes high-quality Arabic instruction available in locations where it did not previously exist, but it also distributes the cost of this expensive resource across a whole network of participating institutions, making it affordable. Thus, the Network's lead professor, Dr. Nabil Abdelfattah, teaches introductory and intermediate Modern Standard Arabic to students across the nation from an interactive video classroom in San Francisco.

However, the Network is not just a distance delivery system. Rather, it configures several resources for language learning into a package of integrated instructional elements. Two additional major resources are critical to USADLN: native Arabic-speaking students and study abroad.

The large group of international students enrolled at U.S. colleges and universities is often considered an underutilized educational resource. In the USADLN, young Arabic-speaking students become locally based teaching assistants (TAs). Of course, as discussed above, if simply placed in the front of an Arabic classroom, these students would probably not provide a quality classroom experience, and in any case they could not be relied upon to provide consistently high-quality instruction. However, when these young native speakers are trained, mentored, and supervised by Professor Abdelfattah, the USADLN professor, they become invaluable teaching resources who are directly accessible to the students. They can extend and complement the lead professor's interactive video sessions with traditional, face-to-face instructional sessions.

The last critical language learning resource built into the USADLN's model is study abroad. Language faculty and study abroad administrators often discuss the importance of a study abroad experience in a country where the language is spoken.

Of course, thousands of American students go overseas every year for the primary purpose of language learning. In the majority of cases, however, students go abroad to programs that are not integrated components of the language program at their home institution. In contrast, USADLN strives to build study abroad into its Arabic program in an integrated, seamless fashion.

USADLN students at any of the eight participating campuses can choose from two study abroad options. The first is to take part in summer, semester, or academic-year programs at Al Akhawayn University in Ifrane, Morocco. This highly regarded Moroccan university offers students the opportunity to further their study of Modern Standard Arabic within an Arabic-language environment (albeit, at least outside the classroom, one in which the Moroccan dialect is the primary language), while also continuing to make progress toward their degrees in classes taught in English. USADLN also offers students the option to undertake an intensive, eight-week summer Arabic course in Alexandria, Egypt. Both programs are administered by Montana State University and are offered as one of the fundamental benefits of institutional membership in the Network. Each of these programs is detailed below, and more information is available on the Network website at www.arabicstudies.edu.

In planning the USADLN and putting these components together, administrators used an unusual source for guidance—the franchise business model that operates at McDonald's, Wendy's, and similar businesses. Successful franchised businesses have developed ways to ensure that they provide everything necessary for a franchise owner to produce the same product at any franchise location. A Big Mac at one McDonald's is identical to a Big Mac produced at any other McDonald's. This is a basic principle for the USADLN: we strive to provide all the elements necessary for each participating member to offer an Arabic language program of equal quality, regardless of the host institution. However, a key difference is that while branding is key to success in the corporate franchising model, MSU does not want to brand the USADLN program, but rather to encourage each Network member to offer the Arabic program as its own course.

Putting all these elements together—a remotely located Arabic lecturer and lead professor, an interactive video network connecting the lead professor with all Network campuses, a native Arabic speaker serving as a teaching assistant at each Network campus, and study abroad options in Morocco and Egypt— the structure of the U.S. Arabic Distance Learning Network emerges (see figure 8.1). As indicated, the lead professor provides two hours of live, interactive instruction per week, working with small clusters of a few Network campuses at a time. The local TAs provide an additional two hours of instruction per week, supplementing the lead professor's lectures. In addition, a Desire2Learn (D2L) asynchronous software network provides a communication system that links the lead professor, the TAs, and the students.

Through this innovative structure, students at all USADLN campuses complete the first two semesters of Modern Standard Arabic. For the past two years, second-year Modern Standard Arabic has been offered as an additional option to Network members based on the same model. Students now have the option to continue to study Arabic for a second year at their home campus or in one of the two study abroad options mentioned above, choosing either an intensive summer program in Egypt or Morocco that focuses on Arabic, or a semester or academic-year program in Morocco that combines Arabic with other courses taught in English.

The annual USADLN membership fee is dramatically lower than the cost of providing instruction through a regular faculty position. Currently, USADLN charges each member institution $7,500 per year for all Network services, including:

- The interactive video classroom and other services of the lead professor;
- A TA training program at the start of the academic year;
- The Desire2Learn asynchronous software network; and
- Study abroad program management and administration.

Additional local costs such as TA stipend and IT facilities usage vary, but these generally come to an additional $7,000–$8,000. This brings the total cost for offering the first year of Arabic and the optional study abroad programs to about $15,000. USADLN members charge their students tuition for the Arabic class at regular rates, enabling them to recoup most, if not all, of these expenses.

The USADLN, now celebrating its 10th year in operation, is well established and tested. Over this period, more than 2,500 students have studied Arabic through the Network program. While success, of course, varies, many students have achieved proficiency levels of intermediate mid and intermediate high on the American Council for the Teaching of Foreign Languages (ACTFL) Arabic proficiency examination after the first year. This represents a significant level of achievement—by definition, according to ACTFL, intermediate-mid speakers are "…able to handle successfully a variety of uncomplicated communicative tasks in straightforward social situations," and intermediate-high speakers are "…able to converse with ease and confidence when dealing with most routine tasks and social situations of the Intermediate level" (www.languagetesting.com).

Network History

MSU realized that if it was struggling to find an affordable way to add more languages to its curriculum, especially less commonly taught languages, other institutions were probably facing the same challenge. Spurred on by this supposition, MSU proceeded to approach institutions in the "heartland of America" with the idea of forming an Arabic language consortium. The response was good. In 1998, a group of like-minded institutions led by MSU submitted two joint proposals. The first proposal was submitted to the National Security Education Program (NSEP) of the U.S. Department of Defense for funds to help implement the new hybrid model for delivering Arabic instruction to multiple institutions. Later in the Network's history, another proposal was submitted to the Comprehensive Program of the U.S. Department of Education, Fund for the Improvement of Secondary Education (FIPSE) to move the Network to self-sustainability, and to apply the model to other languages. In 2002, MSU received the Institute of International Education's Andrew Heiskell Award for Innovation in International Education for demonstrating that institutions could leverage available resources to bring quality Arabic instruction to students at multiple institutions across the country.

After successfully securing NSEP funds, MSU led the implementation phase of the proposed model. MSU's Office of International Programs partnered with the MSU Department of Modern Languages and the MSU Burns Technology Center to form the administrative, academic, and technical hub of the program. This hub has provided the Network leadership, stability, and a home from which to evolve. The Network also engaged a five-member national advisory council with expertise in various facets of Arabic language instruction and distance education. During the formative years of the consortium, this council met on a regular basis with members of MSU's leadership, faculty from partner institutions, the Network professor, the teaching assistants, students, and faculty and administration from the foreign university partner. In fact, one of the early advisory council meetings was held at Al Akhawayn University in Ifrane, Morocco, to help ensure that the U.S.-based Elementary Arabic curriculum and the Intermediate curriculum being developed in Morocco for incoming study abroad students would be a seamless fit.

In the early years of the project, instruction originated from the University of Washington with oversight provided by the Near Eastern Center for Languages. This arrangement proved to be positive, giving the new program a sound instructional foundation and easy access to a major node on the nascent national broadband network committed to university usage. The less than ideal component of this arrangement was that the UW instructional calendar operated on the quarter system, and MSU and the partner institutions used a semester-based calendar. After the project developed a strong curriculum adapted for both distance education and in-class instruction, the advisory council assisted the Network in recruiting a new professor who was not following a quarter-based instructional model.

Another challenge in the early years of the project was the high cost of connecting interactive video classrooms at MSU with those at UW and partner institutions. During the first year of the project, instruction was distributed through dial-up teleconferencing. The cost to the project for phone line charges and bridging fees came to almost $45,000 for two semesters of instruction. Fortunately, the Network has benefitted from leaps in technology and no longer relies on transmitting expensive compressed video over phone lines to deliver instruction. MSU and Network member institutions were among the first universities in the country to utilize Internet2, a networking consortium led by the research and education community that began in 1996, to support interactive video instruction. Currently, connectivity costs are largely absorbed by university subscriptions to the Internet2 network. Costs to the project are based primarily on internal university pricing structures, which up to this time have resulted in minimal or no costs to the project. This situation may change as universities struggle to cover institutional overhead expenses.

The Model in Detail

The Network has retained essentially the same basic structure throughout its tenure, aside from changing where instruction originates and benefitting from lowered overhead expenses related to the more affordable Internet2 delivery system. This model relies on academic, administrative, and technical personnel at multiple institutions working together in virtual and traditional environments, all supported and coordinated by a central administrative and technical hub. This joint effort has resulted in hundreds of students learning elementary and intermediate Arabic every year for the last ten years, most of whom would not have had access to Arabic if not for this Network. The model is described in detail below, and represented in figure 8.1.

FIGURE 8.1: VISUALIZATION OF THE U.S. ARABIC DISTANCE LEARNING NETWORK STRUCTURE

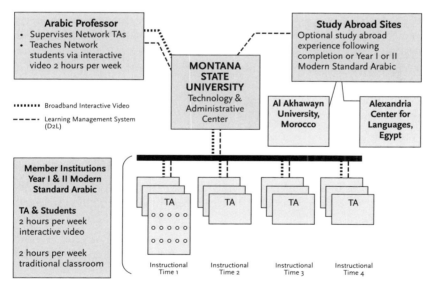

The Professor

The Network professor is an adjunct associate professor in the Department of Modern Languages at MSU. Because of the virtual nature of the program, however, the professor has had the option of living in San Francisco. He delivers instruction from San Francisco State University and is supported by the SFSU technical team to ensure quality audio and visual transmissions to participating institutions across the country. The professor provides the academic grounding for the Network. He creates the course syllabus; trains, supervises, and mentors the teaching assistants; teaches the students two times per week via interactive video; and engages with the TAs and the students through Desire2Learn on a continual basis. Although the professor did not have experience in teaching in a virtual environment prior to joining the Network, in a short period of time he became an expert in adapting his teaching abilities to interactive video and asynchronous learning management system environments. Students consistently give him high evaluations as demonstrated in online evaluations submitted at the end of the semester.

The Teaching Assistants

Partner institutions are responsible for hiring on-site teaching assistants. The TAs attend each video class taught by the professor and are responsible for teaching the traditional classroom sessions held on alternating days. Even though the TAs are critical to students' success in learning Arabic, few have had any formal previous experience in language teaching. More important than previous teaching experience is that the TAs be native speakers of Arabic, have the ability to engage with gregarious American students, and have an enthusiasm for sharing their language and culture. TAs with these characteristics are brought to MSU prior to the start of the academic year for an intensive training workshop at which the professor teaches them about ACTFL-based outcomes in reading, speaking, writing, and listening and how the students will attain these skills through two semesters of instruction. Topics covered in the workshop include:

- Training Session 1: Overview of the course; Student population; Textbooks and supplementary materials; Videoconferencing protocols and demonstration; Objectives of the course; Course syllabus and policies; Q&A.

- Training Session 2: General principles of language proficiency; Guidelines for teaching the alphabet; Guidelines for teaching speaking; Guidelines for teaching writing; Q&A.

- Training Session 3: Testing and evaluation; The role of D2L and demonstration; Classroom management; Weekly schedule; Cultural curriculum and activities; Study abroad; Q&A.

- Training Session 4: Guidelines for a successful class; Inter-Group and Intra-Group communications; Expectations/division of labor—the professor and TAs; Contingency plans for technology malfunctions; Individual and group correspondence—professor, TAs, students; Wrap-up; Q&A.

Since the TAs originate from all parts of North Africa and the Middle East and thus speak various dialects, an important program protocol is that only Modern Standard

Arabic (MSA) be taught in the classroom. The lesson plans are sent electronically to the TAs each week and are all geared to teaching MSA in a standardized manner. Since students throughout the Network take the same quizzes and exams, having a standard curriculum taught in the same sequence and method is important to the students' learning experience. The professor's interactive lectures are complemented by the in-class speaking, reading, writing, and listening exercises designed by the professor but led by the TAs with the professor's guidance and coaching. At mid-year, the professor and the TAs gather in an interactive video session to discuss outcomes of the previous semester and prepare for the next.

Some TAs have enjoyed teaching Arabic to American students so much that there has been an unanticipated program outcome: a few Network TAs have been inspired to pursue teaching Arabic as a career. After earning an engineering degree, one TA enrolled in a linguistics program and is now the primary Arabic lecturer at his institution. At a different institution, the TA completed a PhD program and was hired by another Network member as an Arabic instructor. Sadly, the Network lost two partner institutions to this phenomenon but on the positive side it inadvertently added to the pool of much-needed Arabic instructors in the United States. Another Network TA served as a program coordinator at the U.S. Department of State, Critical Language Scholarships for Intensive Summer Language Institutes (CAORC) program in Yemen, and others have become effective lay translators and tutors in their communities.

The Partner Universities

Network partners have included land-grant institutions, small private liberal arts colleges, historically black colleges and universities, and, for the first time next year, a community college. The common denominator is that all are looking for a way to bring an affordable, high-quality Arabic instructional program to their campus. Some perceive the program as a stepping stone as they test the waters to see if there is enough student interest to justify hiring a tenure-track professor, or as a way to offer Arabic until a qualified Arabic professor can be hired. Other institutions have been with the Network since its inception, and see it as a long-term solution for offering on-campus elementary and intermediate Arabic courses and study abroad options to their students. Still others see this as a way of offering elementary Arabic while freeing up on-campus faculty to teach advanced courses in Arabic language and complementary literature and cultural courses. For the minimal financial investment of the annual membership fee, the teaching assistant salary and support to attend the MSU training workshop, and video classroom and tech fees if they exist, the institution is able to offer, through its own language department and with its own course name and numbering, an Arabic course that captures course tuition for each enrolled student.

Once the partner institution decides to become a Network member, it signs a consortium agreement that spells out the responsibilities of the lead institution and the partner institution. The partner designates personnel who will provide on-campus support, one for academic oversight (the coordinator) and another for technical support (the tech). The coordinator, with administrative support and guidance from MSU, synchronizes the partner institution's academic calendar with the Network's calendar, confirms and publicizes class times, reserves campus classrooms, orders textbooks, recruits students, hires the TA, arranges for the TA's travel to the training workshop, monitors the progress of the course during the academic year, and helps facilitate the study abroad selection process. The tech reserves the distance education classroom and confirms equipment compatibility and integrity of audio/visual connectivity in cooperation with the MSU technical team.

Study Abroad

Network students are encouraged to consider an immersion experience at either Al Akhawayn University (AUI) in Morocco or the Alexandria Centre for Languages (ACL) in Egypt. During the fall semester, the MSU study abroad coordinator, a former student of the Arabic class who studied at AUI for two semesters and traveled extensively throughout the Arab world, attends an interactive video session to share her experience of studying, living, and traveling in North Africa and the Middle East. Students have the opportunity to ask questions about costs, credits, housing, gender issues, travel, risk, safety, and curriculum. Each year the Network sends at least nine and up to 20 students to study at AUI and ACL. Most students opt for the summer program and spend 6–8 weeks in Morocco or Egypt. They study Modern Standard Arabic and take a course in the local dialect to facilitate communications with people they meet in their neighborhoods and on trips to the countryside.

Prior to the students arriving at their study site, the professor has a discussion with instructors at the foreign sites. He informs them of where the students "left off" and briefly describes the strengths and weaknesses of the incoming students. The students bring their texts along and are ready to continue their studies in an integrated, seamless program.

Because students often report that scholarship support makes the difference between being able to study abroad or not, the Network seeks support from foundations and government sources to help increase the number of students benefiting from an in-country experience. The Network was successful in obtaining an $81,600 grant from the IFSA Foundation to support study abroad scholarships for students to study in Morocco and Egypt. In 2007, a program officer from the U.S. Department of State, Critical Language Scholarships for Intensive Summer Language Institutes (CAORC) program was invited to attend a Network interactive video class to make a presentation about their program. Current CAORC information continues to be posted to D2L. As a result, every year several Network students are recipients of CAORC awards to study on fully funded programs. These students have studied Modern Standard Arabic and dialects in Yemen, Morocco, Tunisia, and Egypt.

The Students' Profiles and Accomplishments

There is no typical or dominant USADLN student profile. In contrast to students studying Arabic at universities on the East and West Coasts, where many students are planning to apply their Arabic skills to government or military service, USADLN students studying Arabic at primarily "heartland" institutions often have a different focus. Most students plan to continue in their major and combine acquired Arabic language skills with their intended career track. Over the years, the Arabic class has been composed of students majoring in business, history, political science, international studies, pre-med, atmospheric studies, engineering, teacher education, architecture, religious studies, agriculture, and film. There is also a regular subset of heritage learners. Below are some examples of how USADLN students have applied their language; their names have been changed.

The Agriculturalist

Tony was a lost student. A farm boy not quite sure why he enrolled in college, not quite sure what he wanted to do with his life. He signed up for Arabic because it sounded cool. It grabbed him. He finished one year of Arabic, studied abroad in Morocco, then found his way to Syria. He studied Arabic for a short time in Damascus, then traveled into the countryside, knocked on the door of a farmer and asked if he could work on his farm for the remainder of the summer, which he did. When he returned to the U.S. he applied for and was accepted to a PhD program in agriculture. He was told that one of the reasons the review committee accepted him into the program was because of the initiative his Arabic studies and experience in the Middle East demonstrated.

The Doctor

Justin was a driven student. Always excelling, always stretching. After a year of Arabic he went to Morocco for a summer study abroad program. His parents, brothers, and sisters came to visit him, to the amazement and delight of his friends who took them all home to rural Morocco. After a second year of Arabic, he applied to a U.S. medical school that offered the opportunity to work in a clinic in the West Bank, where he got to use his language skills with Arab patients.

The Architect

Carol's parents met in Morocco; her middle name is Medina. After finishing her master's in architecture, she returned to MSU. When she discovered Arabic was now offered, she felt destined to learn it. After a year she studied abroad in Morocco, first at the exchange university, then at a small language school in the medina of Fes. While studying, she also found time to work on a historical restoration project in the old city. She has since secured title to a kasbah in the south of Morocco and is working with people in the local village and students from MSU to create a local resource center that will house a regional library and classrooms for literacy programs.

The Professor

Jim is a political science major interested in the broader world. Arabic seemed like the natural thing to study. After a year of Arabic he enrolled in the summer abroad program in Alexandria, Egypt. He was learning so much Arabic that he didn't want to leave; he extended his stay at the language center for another semester. He is currently investigating Arabic PhD programs and wants to teach Arabic.

The Engineer

Rebecca studied one year of Arabic in Butte, Montana, and then studied abroad for a summer in Alexandria, Egypt. Her dream is to build roller coasters in the Middle East. Since she is only a junior in engineering, the project is on hold.

The students who study Arabic through the Network sometimes comment that they would prefer having a professor in the classroom, but that they understand that their university would not be able to offer Arabic at this time if not for the distance learning program. Several have actually expressed gratitude at having this option and quickly adapted to the distance learning model. Students who have previous experience with distance education adapt immediately. To complement the interactive video lessons and the TA-led sessions, teaching assistants often organize extramural cultural activities, including film nights, cooking lessons, and soccer games, which enhance the student-TA relationship and give a broader context for language learning. These events often attract students from outside the language course, thus adding to the internationalization of the campus and serving as a course recruitment tool. The MSU Office of International Programs supports these activities by drawing on small budgets for food or film rentals.

Cultural activities have also been supported by mini-grant programs. MSU's application to the Fulbright Visiting Scholar: Direct Access to the Muslim World competition was successful in bringing a Moroccan scholar, Dr. Khalid Bekkaoui, to MSU for 6 weeks. During this time, Dr. Bekkaoui made a significant contribution to the Arabic program. He participated in interactive video lectures, posted cultural materials to the asynchronous course website, moderated discussions after screenings of the films *Control Room* and *Ali Zaoua*, made a presentation to community members and students called "What Muslims Need Americans to Know about Them," and contributed to a seminar on peace and security issues in the Muslim world. The Network encourages all partners to supplement the academic program with such programs and when possible to share the resource via the video sessions or through D2L.

Proficiency Outcomes

Due to limited resources, the Network has not been able to implement proficiency testing for every student enrolled in the program. However, each year a sampling of students is tested. This set includes all students intending to study abroad and a random set of additional students, bringing the total number of students tested up to at least 20. Oral proficiency results for this group have demonstrated that after one year of instruction, students can reach the program's target proficiency level of novice high on the ACTFL proficiency scale. For instance, one year 35 percent of Network students were given an ACTFL proficiency exam, yielding the following results:

TABLE 8.1: ACTFL PROFICIENCY OF NETWORK STUDENTS AFTER ONE YEAR OF ARABIC INSTRUCTION

ACTFL Proficiency Level	#
Novice Low	0
Novice Mid	4
Novice High	4
Intermediate Low	8
Intermediate Mid	3
Intermediate High	3
Advanced Low	1
Advanced Mid	0
Advanced High	0
Superior	1
Distinguished	0

It has been even more challenging to test students after their study abroad experience. But with the recent development of efficient and reliable online proficiency-testing tools for Arabic, the Network hopes to capture more data on student proficiency levels after one year of instruction and after two years of instruction, either through the campus programs or the study abroad experiences.

Network Sustainability

As stated earlier, the Arabic program originated with funding from NSEP and FIPSE. Without this funding, it would have been impossible to develop, implement, test and improve the model, especially in the formative years when distance education technologies were exorbitantly expensive. For the past five years, however, the Network has been self-supporting. Membership fees have covered Network overhead expenses.

Conclusion

If U.S. higher education is going to respond to the challenges of the 21st century, new approaches to language instruction need to be developed that provide quality instruction based on a cost structure that is affordable given current budget constraints. The USADLN has tried to develop just such a new approach, with the aim of making Arabic accessible to students across the fabric of higher education, from community colleges to private institutions to public research universities. Based on its ten-year track record, the Network has proven itself as a way to expand Arabic instruction. Given this success, the Network's approach is likely to prove successful when applied to other less commonly taught languages. Making these additional languages more accessible will be the next challenge for the Network.

The Fulbright Foreign Language Teaching Assistant Program

Educators who are interested in joining the U.S. Arabic Distance Learning Network but do not have locally based students to utilize should be aware of an excellent resource for obtaining native-speaking TAs: the Fulbright Foreign Language Teaching Assistant (FLTA) Program, sponsored by the U.S. Department of State, Bureau of Educational and Cultural Affairs. Each year, U.S. embassies and Fulbright commissions recruit more than 100 native Arabic-speaking TAs from 15 countries in the Middle East and North Africa to study, teach, and serve as cultural ambassadors across the United States. The Fulbright grant covers the cost of housing and a monthly stipend for each FLTA, keeping institution cost-share to a minimum. The only financial responsibility for host institutions is to arrange for the TA to take courses on a credit or audit basis at no cost. A recent survey found that 96 percent of community colleges, large, small, private, and public schools across the United States currently participating believe that instruction has been strengthened at their institution as a result of hosting a Fulbright FLTA and would recommend the program to another institution. For information on how to apply, visit www.flta.fulbrightonline.org

Appendix

Supporting Higher Education in the Middle East and North Africa: IIE's Role and Work in the MENA Region

Elizabeth Khalifa, Director, IIE/MENA Regional Center
Daniel Obst, Deputy Vice President for International Partnerships, IIE

Around the globe, the Institute of International Education (IIE) works to develop global leaders, internationalize higher education, and rescue scholars with the goal of encouraging peace, prosperity, and scientific progress worldwide. Within this work, the renowned Fulbright Program, which IIE has the honor to administer on behalf of the U.S. Department of State, remains one of the most effective and responsive components of U.S. public diplomacy, continuously expanding to serve new academic and community partners.

In recent years, IIE has undertaken a number of strategic initiatives in the Middle East, made possible through public and private investments in higher education and training in such countries as Saudi Arabia, the United Arab Emirates, Qatar, Jordan, and Egypt. These opportunities translate into life-changing experiences for tomorrow's leaders, increase research and teaching capacity across the region, and encourage civic engagement and mutual understanding. They are critical to promoting workforce development, good governance, and gender equity, and they are utilizing social media to connect emerging leaders worldwide to forge solutions to critical problems.

In addition to implementing a number of strategic, large-scale scholarship and training programs in the region, IIE strengthens and links institutions of higher education, conducts research on student mobility to inform educational policy, and provides opportunities for joint learning and exchange of ideas, leveraging its worldwide network of experts and leaders in higher education. Through conferences, study tours, and forums for higher education leaders, IIE brings leaders and educators together to engage students in international research and learning that will improve their knowledge of the world.

The following sections provide a brief overview of the highlights and impacts of just a few of the programs implemented by the Institute's global network, including IIE's MENA Regional Office based in Cairo, Egypt.

Promoting Mutual Understanding: Scholar and Student Exchange Programs

A uniquely effective, global, and flexible form of public diplomacy, the Fulbright Program enables participants from diverse cultural, ethnic, and economic backgrounds to create ties of understanding and respect between the United States and other countries. The program is sponsored by the Bureau of Educational and Cultural Affairs (ECA) of the U.S. Department of State, with additional funding from foreign governments, higher education institutions, and private sector partners and donors. IIE and its Council for International Exchange of Scholars (CIES) have been proud partners in the Fulbright Program since its inception in 1946. Last year, the Fulbright Student Program granted over 100 awards for Americans to study in the Middle East/North Africa; 136 awards were granted to Foreign Fulbright students to pursue studies in the United States. In the Fulbright Scholar program, 55 grants were made to U.S. scholars to teach and conduct research in the Middle East and North Africa region; in addition, 64 visiting scholars and specialists came to the United States from the MENA region.

Since 2003, the Fulbright Visiting Specialists Program, Direct Access to the Muslim World, has helped U.S. higher education institutions and communities enrich their understanding of Islamic civilization and culture, as well as their knowledge of social, political, and economic developments in countries with significant Muslim populations. Last year, 15 Fulbright Visiting Specialists were matched with U.S. institutions for a period of three to six weeks to lecture or teach short courses, assist with program and curriculum development, interact with students, and participate in public outreach programs.

The Fulbright Foreign Language Teaching Assistant (FLTA) Program supports more than 100 native Arabic-speaking Teaching Assistants each year from 15 countries in the Middle East and North Africa to study, teach, and serve as cultural ambassadors at higher education institutions across the United States.

The Hubert H. Humphrey Fellowship Program, funded by the Bureau of Educational and Cultural Affairs of the U.S. Department of State, provides a year of professional enrichment in the United States for experienced professionals from designated countries, including many in the MENA region. Each year approximately 200 Fellows are selected based on their potential for leadership and their commitment to public service in either the public or private sector, and engage in nondegree study and related professional experiences at selected American universities.

In summer 2010, IIE will bring Iraqi scholars for short-term visits to U.S. campuses through the Fulbright Visiting Scholar Program for Iraq. This program is administered by IIE's Council for International Exchange of Scholars (CIES) on behalf of the U.S. Department of State.

Promoting Study Abroad in the Region

By administering some of the world's most prestigious and innovative scholarship programs, the Institute is providing talent from around the world with access to leading institutions of higher education and the international experience that is critical to success in the 21st-century workplace. These programs are vital in promoting international dialogue and mutual understanding. They provide opportunities for international students to study in the U.S. and other countries and promote study abroad for U.S. students, especially those who may lack the necessary financial means. Central to achieving these goals are the Benjamin A. Gilman International Scholarships, administered on behalf of the U.S. Department of State, and the David L. Boren Scholarships, administered on behalf of the National Security Education Program.

The Gilman Program offers grants for U.S. citizen undergraduate students of limited financial means to pursue academic studies abroad. Last year, nearly 100 students studied abroad in the MENA region with support from the Gilman Program, including in Egypt, Morocco, and Jordan. The Boren Scholarships and Fellowships provide unique funding opportunities for U.S. undergraduate and graduate students to add an important international and language component to their educations, focusing on geographic areas, languages, and fields of study that are critical to U.S. interests and underrepresented in study abroad. Nearly 100 Boren Scholarships and Fellowships were awarded for study in the MENA region this year.

The Ibrahim Leadership and Dialogue Project in the Middle East is another unique initiative, managed by IIE for the Ibrahim Family Foundation. The program provides U.S. undergraduate students of diverse backgrounds with the opportunity to participate in a 10-day study tour in three Middle Eastern countries, including United Arab Emirates, Saudi Arabia, Jordan, and Israel. Students interact with leaders and organizations working to promote dialogue and mutual understanding.

Recently, IIE, in cooperation with the Hollings Center, convened senior educators from the United States and 10 Arab countries at Al Akhawayn University in Ifrane, Morocco to discuss issues related to increasing U.S. study abroad in the region, including institutional capacity, academic standards, cross-cultural issues, and perceptions of safety and security. The findings from the workshop were published in a white paper that can be downloaded at www.iie.org. And in May 2010, IIE published a new directory of study abroad programs, *IIEPassport Study Abroad in the Middle East and Africa*. This directory was produced in collaboration with Lonely Planet and includes hundreds of study abroad program listings in the region.

Managing Scholarship Programs

IIE works with corporations and foundations to provide scholarships to talented individuals from around the world to study abroad in specialized fields that will build a skilled workforce in their home countries and contribute to local community development.

To train petroleum professionals in health, safety, and environmental protection and lay the foundation for future international cooperation, Libya's Waha Oil Company partnered with IIE to create a scholarship program that brings its employees to U.S. universities for intensive study of English and advanced training in geology, petroleum engineering, oil production, and business management. IIE also partners with Zueitina Oil Company and Petro Canada to deliver similar programs.

On behalf of ExxonMobil, IIE manages fully funded scholarships for student leaders to receive graduate degrees in geosciences at universities in the United States. IIE monitored 75 students studying in the U.S. and Europe from Russia, Indonesia, and over a dozen countries in the MENA region, including Algeria, Bahrain, Egypt, Iraq, Jordan, Kuwait, Lebanon, Libya, Morocco, Oman, Qatar, Saudi Arabia, Tunisia, and United Arab Emirates.

Driving Innovation in Higher Education in the Middle East

IIE is using its global network to administer scholarship programs and identify outstanding students for academic institutions in the MENA region. IIE is assisting New York University in identifying the first cohort of scholarship recipients for NYU Abu Dhabi. More than 100 of the finest graduating high school students from around the world are being chosen to join the inaugural freshman class when the new campus opens in the fall of 2010. This endeavor strengthens and advances IIE's goal of opening minds to the world by establishing a unique intellectual community that brings together students of different backgrounds, builds their leadership capacity, and develops truly global citizens.

Since May 2007, IIE has also worked with King Abdullah University of Science and Technology in Saudi Arabia to identify outstanding students globally to receive scholarships to pursue advanced degrees in science, technology, and engineering. KAUST's first 368 students come from more than 46 countries. They are studying in 11 fields, including applied mathematics and computational science, earth sciences and engineering, and mechanical engineering. As a coeducational, graduate-level research university, KAUST is dedicated to inspiring a new era of scientific achievement that will benefit the region and the world.

Leadership Development

IIE believes that young minds are critical to bringing creative solutions and new energy to the complex challenges facing our world. Through leadership programs that engage students from schools, youth centers, and undergraduate institutions in the Middle East and North Africa, IIE helps young people develop their leadership styles and prepares them for civic involvement and conflict resolution. These programs expose students to different leadership approaches, provide space for them to explore their values and visions, and help them build critical skill sets such as teamwork, communication, creativity, networking, and project planning. Students also experience leadership through interaction with community leaders and service learning opportunities.

The IIE MENA Regional Office and Center for Leadership Excellence in Cairo works with individuals and institutions that recognize the critical need for leadership capacity building. The Center provides innovative leadership programs to diverse audiences including organizations, professionals, and youth. Initiatives include the Discovery Program, the Youth Enrichment for Leadership Learning and Action (YELLA) program, the USAID Peace Scholarships Program, and the Entrepreneurial Leadership Program for Egyptian Women.

The Discovery National Student Leadership Program, a semester-long initiative sponsored by the Ford Foundation and the Stuart Foundation, is currently in its seventh full-semester iteration in Egypt, and now counts over 160 alumni. Alumni are entering the workforce with employable skills and confidence, and are pioneers in understanding new and effective leadership approaches. With support from the U.S. Department of State, the Youth Enrichment for Leadership Learning and Action (YELLA) program provides some 15 Egyptian preparatory and secondary schools and youth centers with a curriculum of leadership learning lessons that builds the capacity of the schools to deliver youth leadership programming in the future.

The USAID-funded Peace Scholarships Program, administered in partnership with World Learning, provides leadership learning and U.S. study abroad opportunities to Arab students from across the region. Competitively selected university students from Algeria, Egypt, Jordan, Lebanon, Morocco, Oman, West Bank, and Yemen participate in leadership institutes through IIE centers in Cairo and Denver, and attend U.S. universities for one year of academic study.

Professional Development

Building leadership skills and enhancing the capacity of individuals and organizations to address local and global challenges are vital parts of IIE's mission. The long- and short-term training programs arranged by the Institute connect students and professionals with peers and colleagues around the world to gain the skills and international perspectives they will need to forge solutions to global challenges.

IIE works with world-class trainers and facilitators to deliver professional development programs that meet the strategic and performance enhancement needs of institutions in the region. Over 20 corporations, foundations, and government entities based in the region currently benefit from IIE professional programs, which also serve the U.S. Department of State's International Visitor Leadership Program.

One example is IIE's recent work with the Jordanian House of Deputies. "The Role of Legislators in the Democratic Process" was a two-week program, sponsored by the Public Affairs Section at the Embassy of the United States in Amman, Jordan, that introduced 10 newly elected members of the Jordanian House of Deputies to the structure and process of legislating in the United States at the local, state, and federal levels of government, with an emphasis on the federalist system and separation of powers.

Women's Empowerment Programs

The Institute is committed to providing leadership training to underserved groups. Increasing women's effectiveness as leaders in the public and private sectors is critical to achieving wide-scale gender equity around the world.

Since its launch in 2005, Women in Technology (WIT) has impacted the lives of more than 7,000 women in the Middle East and North Africa (MENA). With funding from the U.S. Department of State and Microsoft and in collaboration with local partners in nine countries, IIE helped 60 women's organizations provide business planning, professional development, and information technology skills to women in their communities. In 2009 alone, Women in Technology (WIT) trained more than 2,500 women in the MENA region through its unique model of collaboration between government and the private sector.

Sponsored by Susan G. Komen for the Cure, the Global Initiative for Breast Cancer Awareness works to create a global network of dedicated activists with the skills to play a strategic role in shaping their country's response to breast cancer. The first phase of the Global Initiative trained nearly 600 individuals representing 24 communities in 8 countries, including Jordan, Saudi Arabia, and United Arab Emirates. With USAID support, the Global Initiative expanded to implement the Course for the Cure in Egypt in partnership with local organizations. The course trains women to perform community assessments and advocate for breast health and cancer awareness. In 2009, the program launched a community grants initiative that supported 37 innovative and collaborative projects, many of which were leveraged with financial support from local organizations in the host countries.

The Entrepreneurial Leadership Program for Egyptian Women is designed for women entrepreneurs and female high school students to build awareness and create linkages that will contribute to the growth of entrepreneurship for women in Egypt. The program, funded by the Stuart Family Foundation, is designed to provide linkages between these two target groups and opportunities for practical skill building and exchange on themes related to entrepreneurship, leadership, and other success factors.

Rebuilding Higher Education in Iraq

The Institute is also committed to helping to rebuild Iraq's higher education system, in particular through linkages with U.S. universities and programs to assist threatened scholars. Since 2007, IIE's Scholar Rescue Fund has helped relocate over 200 threatened academics in Iraq to host institutions in the region where they can continue their academic work in freedom and safety. An important part of this project is providing Iraqi scholars with professional development and e-learning tools so that they can enhance their skills and also keep in close contact with academic communities back home. The aim of the program is to keep threatened scholars safe, help them build their academic and professional skills, and assist them to return home so that they can contribute to rebuilding higher education in Iraq as soon as it is safe for them to do so.

The Institute continues to expand its work in the Middle East and North Africa, a region where international education and training programs promise great potential to benefit not just the fortunate, but also the thousands of marginalized individuals whose talents are critical to their countries' development. To learn more about IIE's programs, please visit www.iie.org/MENA.

Appendix

Classifying Higher Education Institutions in the MENA Region: A Pilot Project

Rajika Bhandari, Deputy Vice President, Research and Evaluation, IIE
Robert Gutierrez, Senior Manager, Research and Evaluation, IIE

While several international-level ranking systems and as many as 20 country-level ranking and classification systems exist around the world, a regional classification of higher education institutions in the Middle East and North Africa (MENA) region has not been developed to date. Such a system is particularly needed given the rapid expansion of the higher education sector in the region, which has recently seen the appearance of new domestic institutions as well as branch campuses of overseas institutions.

In several countries, rankings have come to occupy an important place in the higher education sector, influencing student applications, funding, graduate recruitment, and public policy. As higher education discourse has shifted from local to global, with universities seen as critical to preparing globally competitive citizens, rankings too have become more globalized, and several current efforts compare institutions across the world. In recent years, perhaps the best-known worldwide rankings have been the Shanghai Jiao Tong University rankings and the Times Higher Education–QS World University Rankings.

Although they provide an easy metric by which to compare higher education institutions, rankings have received a great deal of criticism. Research has increasingly shown that although rankings are useful snapshots of world-class institutions, they typically suffer from several flaws, including subjective assessment criteria, a bias towards the natural sciences, cultural biases, an over-reliance on peer review and the use of subjective opinions of respondents unfamiliar with institutions in other world regions, and constantly shifting indicators and criteria that make long-term comparisons impossible. In addition, comparisons across ranking systems are difficult, as each uses a different set of weighted indicators or metrics to measure higher education activity.

Recognizing a significant need for reliable and accurate institution-level data on higher education institutions in the MENA region, the Institute of International Education (IIE) recently received support from the Carnegie Corporation of New York to develop, on a pilot basis, a system for assessing and classifying higher education institutions in the MENA region. This short chapter provides an introduction to this new project and an update on its current status and partnership with the Lebanese Association for Educational Studies (LAES).

Purpose of Project

The project's primary goal is to develop a new classification system that will better inform the global higher education community and provide a deeper understanding of the region's diverse range of institutions and their characteristics. The project will aim to include a representative makeup of the region among its focus countries, which will include Egypt, Lebanon, Jordan, Saudi Arabia, Qatar, UAE, Morocco, and Tunisia.

With coordination from LAES as a local partner, the project team will aim to develop a classification system for higher education institutions in the MENA region, using key academic and internationalization indicators. Because of the inherent limitations of a ranking approach, the focus of the study is to identify a set of relevant and objective indicators that can be used to describe institutions in the MENA region, rather than to develop a rigid ranking system that yields a single hierarchical list of institutions.

Two key advantages to developing a classification or typology for the MENA region as opposed to a ranking system are that the classification approach accounts for key differences among higher education institutions, and that classifications help identify meaningful similarities and differences among institutions without necessarily making a judgment about quality. In contrast, in their reductionist approach, rankings often disregard the fact that higher education institutions can differ significantly in mission, history, and size, and that it is often meaningless to reduce these variations into a single score or rank.

Anticipated Outcomes of the Project

The project will help to strengthen MENA institutions locally by providing benchmarks and key indicators against which they will be able to measure their growth, as well as a means to compare themselves to similar institutions. The new classification system will also help generate international interest in the region's institutions—which supports a secondary goal of the project, which is to deepen linkages between MENA higher education institutions and other institutions around the world to facilitate knowledge sharing, research collaboration, and institutional capacity building.

Long-term impacts should reveal a greater awareness on the part of MENA institutions and institutions worldwide of the unique characteristics of institutions in the region. The project team also expects to see other indirect long-term impacts, for example: an increase in the number of MENA institutions listed in other global rankings systems, more inter-regional research and exchange collaboration between institutions in MENA countries, and expanded international collaboration with institutions outside the MENA region.

Progress Update and Partners

To date, the project team, led by research staff at IIE, has carried out an extensive literature review and also consulted with a wide variety of experts in the classification and rankings field to identify stakeholders and an appropriate local partner in the MENA region. IIE, as a lead partner in the project, brings over 60 years of experience in collecting institution-level data, including the mobility data published annually in the widely cited *Open Doors: Report on International Educational Exchange*. IIE's research and evaluation capabilities extend into policy research, program evaluation, and other key projects conducted on behalf of governments, foundations, and private sponsors.

IIE's local partner, the Lebanese Association for Educational Studies (LAES), is a nonprofit, nongovernmental organization whose membership consists of 54 members, including academics and researchers in the field of education at Lebanese universities. Dr. Adnan El-Amine, a well-known regional expert on higher education, will lead the association's work on this project. The author of dozens of articles and papers on higher education reform in the Arab world, Dr. El-Amine is a member of the UNESCO national commission for Lebanon, has served as a member of the coordinating committee of the Arab Education Forum, and was a Fulbright Scholar at Boston College in 2005.

Since 1995, LAES has been actively engaged in comprehensive research activities and projects conducted on behalf of ministries of education and higher education in Lebanon and other Arab countries, UNESCO's Regional Bureau for Education in the Arab States, the United Nations Development Programme (UNDP), and the World Bank, among others. In an effort to expand its reach, the Association recently opened its membership to members of non-Lebanese nationalities representing the broader region.

Together with LAES, the project team has identified the specific criteria and key indicators that will be used to collect data on institutional characteristics and internationalization at higher education institutions. Broad categories of indicators include institutional, student body, and faculty characteristics; teaching and learning areas; research, financial resources, and expenses; and internationalization. As an immediate next step, the team will develop survey instruments to be disseminated widely to all institutions via national ministries of higher education, with the aim of producing a report in fall 2011.

For more information about the project, contact:

Rajika Bhandari, PhD
Deputy Vice President of Research and Evaluation
Institute of International Education
rbhandari@iie.org

Robert Gutierrez
Senior Manager, Research and Evaluation
Institute of International Education
rgutierrez@iie.org

Appendix

HISTORICAL TRENDS IN STUDENT MOBILITY FROM THE MIDDLE EAST TO THE UNITED STATES

PATRICIA CHOW, SENIOR PROGRAM OFFICER, RESEARCH AND EVALUATION, IIE
SHEPHERD LAUGHLIN

The number of students from the Middle East studying at colleges and universities in the United States has fluctuated widely over the past 60 years. During the oil boom years in the 1970s and early 1980s, the proportion of international students from the Middle East was quite high—26 percent of the world total in 1980/81 (Bhandari and Chow, 2009). In recent decades, however, far more students have come from countries in East and South Asia, in particular China, India, South Korea, and Japan. During the 2008/09 academic year, for example, more than three times as many students (103,260) came from India as from the entire Middle Eastern region[1] (29,140), according to the annual *Open Doors: Report on International Educational Exchange*. While individual countries in the Middle East may be sending more students to the U.S. on a per capita basis than India, the net result of the lower overall total is less representation at U.S. campuses: Middle Eastern students comprised only 4 percent of all international students in the U.S. in 2008/09, compared to 15 percent each for India and China.

The number of students from the Middle East pursuing higher education in the U.S. declined in the years immediately following 9/11, however, more recently these numbers have rebounded. During the 2008/09 academic year, most countries in the Middle East continued to see a reversal of post-9/11 declines in the number of students choosing to study overseas in the United States. Among the Gulf States, for example, Saudi Arabia saw an increase of 28 percent over the previous year's total to 12,661 students, the United Arab Emirates saw a 24 percent increase to 1,218, and Qatar saw a 34 percent increase to 463. Non-Gulf places of origin also generally saw increases—362 students came from the Palestinian Territories (a 45 percent increase), and 2,225 came from Jordan (a 24 percent increase). In the entire region, only Oman and Syria saw declines, of 25 and 11 percent, respectively.

It may come as a surprise to recall that for almost a decade (1974–1983), Iran was the top country of origin of international students in the U.S.; 51,310 Iranian students were studying in the U.S. during the peak year of 1979/80 (Marcus, 2009).

In 1980/81, there were 10,400 students from Saudi Arabia pursuing higher education in the U.S., a figure surpassed only in 2008/09 after several years of double-digit percentage increases.

The reasons for such dramatic changes relate to a combination of economic factors, international relations, social changes, and government education policy. For example, it has been suggested that Middle Eastern students responded to declines in the price of petroleum in the 1980s by choosing to study in the United States in fewer numbers (figure A.1). The mid- to late 1970s were years of high oil prices, in part due to production quotas imposed by the Organization of Petroleum Exporting Countries (OPEC), which counted Iran as a member. These oil-boom years allowed more students from the region to be supported for study in the United States. When a surplus of oil flooded world markets at the beginning of the 1980s and the price of oil declined, declines were noted in *Open Doors* for Iran and other Middle Eastern countries. However, the declines also correlate with a particularly tense period in U.S.-Iran relations and to changes within Iranian society that may have impacted student mobility, making it difficult to establish a clear causal relationship.

The situation is equally complex in Saudi Arabia. As in Iran, the number of students from Saudi Arabia studying in the U.S. declined throughout the 1980s, which may be related to changes in the price of oil and other outside factors. After steady gains throughout the 1990s, numbers once again declined immediately following 9/11. However, the number of Saudi students in the U.S. has risen 317 percent in four years from a low point of 3,035 in 2004/05 to 12,661 in 2008/09. In this case, the reason for the increases is clear—for the last several years, the Saudi government has financed overseas education for talented young Saudis through the King Abdullah Foreign Scholarship Program. Since its inception in 2006, the program has sent more than 62,000 students to colleges and universities around the world.

FIGURE A.1: NUMBER OF STUDENTS FROM SAUDI ARABIA AND IRAN COMPARED TO THE PRICE OF OIL, 1976/77 TO 2008/09

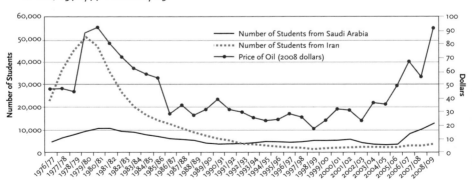

Source: Price of oil data is based on statistics from the Energy Information Administration available at http://tonto.eia.doe.gov and and numbers from 1986 on refer to monthly prices in January. All other data is from *Open Doors*.

The number of students from the Gulf States—defined here as Kuwait, Bahrain, Saudi Arabia, Qatar, United Arab Emirates, and Oman, the six members of the Gulf Cooperation Council—reached a high of 12,704 in 2000/01, before declining to 6,934 in 2004/05. The total then began to increase again, reaching 17,075 in 2008/09. When Saudi Arabia is excluded, the picture is somewhat different. The Gulf total minus Saudi Arabia reached its low point only in 2006/07, at 3,460, before rising to 4,414 in 2008/09. In the Gulf as a whole, post-9/11 declines are being reversed, but this trend is less pronounced throughout the region than figures that include Saudi Arabia would suggest.

FIGURE A.2: STUDENTS FROM GULF STATES STUDYING IN THE U.S., 1999/00 TO 2008/09

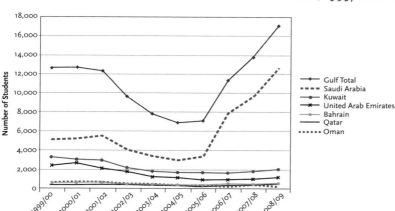

Turkey has been a top place of origin of international students in the United States for over half a century. In 1949/50, 483 students from Turkey were studying in the U.S., a figure comparable with other top places of origin in the region, such as Iran (570) and Iraq (499). However, Turkey was largely unaffected by the declines seen throughout the Middle East during the 1980s, with numbers continuing to increase, from 2,210 in 1979/80 to 3,400 a decade later, and reaching an all-time high of 13,263 in 2008/09. Among notable programs that have drawn Turkish students to the U.S., the State University of New York (SUNY) offers a dual degree program that has enrolled more than 2,000 Turkish students, with 262 graduates, as of the start of the 2008/09 academic year.

FIGURE A.3: STUDENTS FROM TURKEY AND SAUDI ARABIA STUDYING IN THE U.S., 1999/00
TO 2008/09

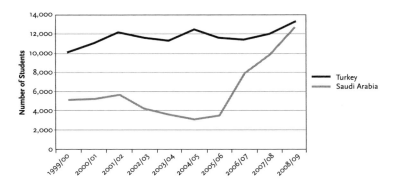

As Middle Eastern countries continue to invest in higher education, hosting more international students, and as more students from all areas of the Middle East continue to study overseas in ever greater numbers, the *Open Doors* statistics in the coming years will likely reflect this changing environment and the many new initiatives currently being established in this region.

[1] In *Open Doors 2009*, Turkey and Cyprus are included in the Europe region, not the Middle East region.

REFERENCES

Bhandari, R., & Chow, P. (2009). *Open Doors 2009: Report on International Educational Exchange*. New York, NY: Institute of International Education.

Marcus, R. (2009, spring). Student flows from the Middle East: Iranian and Saudi Arabian students in the United States. *IIENetworker*, 39–40.

About the Contributors

Haifa Reda Jamal Al-Lail joined Effat University in 1998 and began her tenure as president in May 2008. She is one of the winners of "1,000 Women for the Nobel Peace Prize 2005" and was the winner of the Distinguished Arabian Woman Award in 2005. A respected author and researcher, she is well known for her expertise in privatization and women's empowerment. She is the author of several articles and has developed and taught undergraduate and graduate courses on topics like public administration and public policy. Before joining Effat University, Jamal Al-Lail was the first dean of the girls' campus at King Abdulaziz University. She was a visiting scholar at the John F. Kennedy School of Government in 2001. She participated in the Summer Institute for Women in Higher Education Administration at Bryn Mawr College in 2000. She is a native speaker of Arabic and received a PhD in public policy from the University of Southern California.

Robert G. Ayan Jr. is managing partner at Cambridge Advisors LLC, a Cambridge, Massachusetts–based strategy and management consulting firm that specializes in economic development through integrated approaches to public policy, education, and entrepreneurship, where he currently serves as chief strategist to El Hassan Science City in Amman, Jordan. Previously, Ayan served as the program manager of the MIT Entrepreneurship Center at the Massachusetts Institute of Technology, where he helped entrepreneurs commercialize their innovations. Ayan holds a Master in Business Administration from the MIT Sloan School of Management and a Bachelor of Science in Business Administration from Boston University. He may be reached at ayan@cambridge-advisors.com and www.cambridge-advisors.com.

Rajika Bhandari is deputy vice president of research and evaluation at the Institute of International Education (IIE) in New York, where she leads two major research projects—Open Doors and Project Atlas—that measure international higher education mobility at the domestic (U.S.) and international levels. She is a frequent speaker and author on the topic of mobility, serves on the Global Advisory Council of the Observatory on Borderless Higher Education, and is on the editorial board of the *Journal of Studies in International Education*. Bhandari also conducts evaluations of IIE's international scholarship and fellowship programs. Before joining IIE in 2006, Bhandari was a senior researcher at MPR Associates, an educational research firm in Berkeley, California that provides research and evaluation services to the U.S. Department of Education. She also served as the assistant director for evaluation at the Mathematics and Science Education Network at the University of North Carolina at Chapel Hill. She holds a doctoral degree in psychology from North Carolina State University and a BA (Honors) in psychology from the University of Delhi, India.

Jerome B. Bookin-Weiner joined AMIDEAST as director of study abroad and outreach in October 2007. A specialist in the history of Morocco, he is also well known for his work in international education. A former Fulbright scholar in Morocco, Bookin-Weiner is the author of numerous articles and editor of a book on U.S.-Moroccan relations. He also developed and served as project director for numerous institutional, faculty, and curriculum development projects funded by the U.S. Department of Education and the National Endowment for the Humanities, including one currently underway to develop multimedia teaching materials for Egyptian, Jordanian, Moroccan, and Kuwaiti Arabic. Bookin-Weiner has developed and taught undergraduate and graduate courses on the Third World, the Middle East, and North Africa, and has advised students running more than 30 Model United Nations conferences at three institutions. Before joining AMIDEAST, Bookin-Weiner was vice president for academic affairs at The Scholar Ship and held faculty and administrative positions at Old Dominion University (1976–1987), Bentley College (1987–2001), and Colorado State University (2001–2004). He also served as a Peace Corps volunteer in Morocco, where he taught at the National Forestry School and in the English Department of Mohammed V University. He earned his BA in history at Dickinson College and his MA and PhD in modern Middle East history from Columbia University.

Qianyi Chen is a master's student in the Higher Education Management program at the University of Pittsburgh. She is also a center associate at the Institute for Higher Education Management at the University of Pittsburgh. Chen earned her Bachelor of Arts degree in English literature in China at Sichuan International Studies University. Before pursuing her master's degree, Chen taught English as a second language in a prestigious middle school in Chongqing, China. Her main research interest is comparative higher education, particularly in the area of financing. During her course of study, she has done research about financing in China's higher education institutions. Currently, Chen is working on a comparative study of faculty evaluation of teaching between Chinese and American elite institutions of higher education.

Patricia Chow is a senior program officer in research and evaluation at the Institute of International Education. She serves as the research manager and editor of *Open Doors: Report on International Educational Exchange*. Prior to joining IIE, Patricia worked as an English teacher in Osaka, Japan and conducted research in Europe and Brazil. She is a proud alumna of the University of California, Berkeley and also holds master's degrees from the University of Pennsylvania and New York University.

Hana Addam El-Ghali is a doctoral student at the University of Pittsburgh in the program of Social and Comparative Analysis in Education. El-Ghali is one of two managing directors at the Institute for International Studies in Education at the School of Education. Her background is in education, both teaching and administration. She earned her Bachelor of Arts in elementary education, a diploma in educational management and leadership, and a Master of Arts in educational administration and policy studies in Lebanon at the American University of Beirut. Before pursuing her doctoral studies, El-Ghali taught English as a second language at two local schools in Beirut. Her research interests are in comparative, international, and developing education (CIDE), particularly in higher education in developing countries. Currently, El-Ghali is working on several research projects looking at higher education and youth unemployment in Lebanon and the Middle East.

Sherifa Mohamed B.E. Fayez is the executive national director AFS Egypt. In 2004, Fayez spearheaded the association's restructuring plans as well as growth and development implementation strategies, allowing it to have a presence in 18 cities nationwide. Fayez facilitated the start-up of partner offices promoting intercultural understanding in several countries including Saudi Arabia, Tunisia, Kenya, Morocco, India, and Ghana. Fayez is a graduate of the American University in Cairo in 1986 as an economics major. She is the mother of two AFS exchange students, and her home hosts regularly students and friends from all over the world.

Robert Gutierrez is senior manager of research and evaluation at the Institute of International Education. In this capacity, he has led a number of government- and foundation-supported research projects and program evaluations for sponsors including the U.S. Departments of State and Education, the Carnegie Corporation of New York, and the German Academic Exchange Service (DAAD). He also manages projects related to global student mobility, including Project Atlas, conducts research on U.S. study abroad through the *Meeting America's Global Education Challenge* policy research series, and presents frequently at conferences on international education and exchange. Gutierrez holds an MS in public policy and management from Carnegie Mellon University and a BA in English and Spanish from the University of Notre Dame.

Elizabeth B. Khalifa is currently the MENA Region Director for IIE based in Cairo, Egypt where she provides leadership and managerial oversight for IIE initiatives in the region, including programs under the IIE Center for Leadership Excellence. She is an experienced management, human resources, and training development professional, specializing in the leadership of initiatives that build human capacity. She has held senior management and technical assistance positions in Egypt since 1983 with the Institute of International Education (IIE), AMIDEAST, Chemonics, The American University in Cairo, and private commercial banks. Liz works with a dynamic team of dedicated staff, consultants, and partner institutions to design, implement, and sustain new initiatives including the Student Leadership Discovery Program and the Youth Enrichment for Leadership Learning and Action Program (YELLA), and the Africa Higher Education Collaborative (AHEC). Liz is active in the community, serving on the board of the Binational Fulbright Commission in Egypt and the core working group of American Chamber of Commerce's Education Committee. Liz holds an MBA degree from the New York University Stern School of Business Administration and a BA in international relations from Hobart and William Smith Colleges, Geneva, New York.

Daniel Kirk is currently a faculty member at the American University of Sharjah, where he teaches education courses and directs the Faculty Development Centre. He is also the founding president of the Gulf Comparative Education Society, a membership organization that aims to enhance educational research and discourse in the Gulf and wider Middle East. Kirk spent almost a decade teaching secondary school students English literature and language in schools in England, Qatar, Bermuda, and Dubai. He has served as an external consultant to the Ministry of Education of the United Arab Emirates, and has also worked closely with the American University of Ras al Khaimah (UAE) on a new Master of Education degree in educational leadership and teaching and learning. Kirk received a PhD in language and literacy education from the University of Georgia. He also received a Master of Arts in special education, a Post Graduate Certificate of Education, and a Bachelor of Arts (Honors) degree in English studies, all from the University of Sunderland, England.

Shepherd Laughlin is a freelance editor and writer based in Brooklyn, New York. He was previously a program officer at the New York headquarters of the Institute of International Education, where he worked as a publications editor and program administrator from 2007–2009. While at IIE, he edited several books and reports related to educational mobility, including *U.S.-China Educational Exchange: Perspectives on a Growing Partnership, Higher Education on the Move: New Developments in Global Mobility*, and others. His undergraduate thesis, *Global China, Local Chinas: Modernization and Ethnic Identity in the People's Republic*, was published in 2007 after winning the Brown University Senior Honors Thesis Publication Competition. In 2005, Laughlin traveled to China on a Freeman-ASIA scholarship to study Mandarin, and he later spent time in France studying at Sciences Po. He received an AB with Honors in international relations from Brown University. His website is http://shepherdlaughlin.com

Ahmad Y. Majdoubeh is a professor of English and American literature at the University of Jordan (UJ). He is presently the dean of the newly created Faculty of Foreign Languages. He has recently been selected as a member of the Higher Education Council in Jordan and the Royal Commission on Education. He was director of the Office of International Programs and director of the Language Center at UJ for several years, where he worked closely with incoming American students and those in charge of American study abroad programs. He is also one of Jordan's two experts on the Bologna Process. He writes a weekly article for *Jordan Times*, the national English-language daily, on a variety of subjects, including education. He taught at Yarmouk University in Jordan from 1984–1994, when he transferred to the University of Jordan, where he has been working ever since. He was a visiting research fellow at several international institutions, including the Newberry Library in Chicago, the Ludwig-Maximillian University in Munich, Waseda University in Japan, Yonsei University in South Korea, and Lund University in Sweden. He is the recipient of several grants, from Telluride House, the National Endowment for the Humanities, the Fulbright Summer Institute, DAAD, the Japan Foundation, the Korea Foundation, and the European Commission. He is also a short story writer and an academic leader of several short-term seminars on international education and other subjects. He obtained his BA in 1977 from the University of Jordan, and his MA in 1982 and PhD in 1984 from Cornell University.

Daniel Obst is deputy vice president of international partnerships at the New York headquarters of the Institute of International Education (IIE), one of the largest and oldest not-for-profit organizations in the field of international educational exchange and development training. Obst provides strategic leadership in the creation and implementation of international academic partnerships, and oversees all the activities of IIE's network of 1,000 member institutions, as well as IIE's print publications, online directories, conference, and seminars. He is the editor of *IIENetworker*, IIE's international education magazine, and executive editor of IIE's *Global Education Research Reports* series. Obst recently coedited a new book funded by the EU-U.S. Atlantis Program, *Joint and Double Degree Programs: An Emerging Model for Transatlantic Exchange,* and coauthored two white papers in IIE's series on *Meeting America's Global Education Challenge*. Obst received his BA in international relations from the George Washington University and holds a master's degree in European studies from the London School of Economics.

Norm Peterson is the vice provost for international education at Montana State University. Prior to assuming this position, Peterson served as the founding executive director for the Alliance for International Educational and Cultural Exchange, a Washington, DC–based advocacy coalition representing major education organizations. He has also held international education positions at Georgetown University, the University of Maryland, and the University of Colorado. His additional major professional accomplishments include designing and developing the nationally recognized U.S. Arabic Distance Learning Network, spearheading revisions of federal financial aid rules to expand access of funds for study abroad, leading the 1991 initiative to develop and enact the National Security Education Program, and designing and implementing the administrative structure for the International Student Exchange Program (ISEP). Peterson currently serves as the chair of the AIEA Policy Advisory Board, and is past chair of NAFSA's International Educational Leadership Knowledge Community. He received a PhD in philosophy from the University of Colorado-Boulder.

Dan Prinzing is the education director for the Idaho Human Rights Education Center in Boise, Idaho. A manager of education partnerships and projects throughout the world, Prinzing directs efforts to increase the global perspective of Idaho's students through curriculum integration that focuses on global cultures, global connections, and global issues in the belief that "recognition of the inherent dignity and of the equal and inalienable rights of all members of the human family is the foundation of freedom, justice, and peace in the world." Prinzing has a BA in history secondary education, an MA in curriculum and instruction, an MA in history and government, and a PhD in educational administration. Before his current position, he was the Idaho State Department of Education's coordinator of civic and international education.

Yvonne Rudman is the director for academic and technical programs in the Office of International Programs at Montana State University and the project director for MSU's U.S. Arabic Distance Learning Network. She has managed MSU's award-winning Arabic language program since its inception. Rudman also has extensive experience in managing a wide range of grant-funded, internationally based projects in agriculture, education reform, environmental public health, and business development. She has managed MSU's study abroad exchange programs with over 40 institutions in approximately 20 countries. Rudman has an undergraduate degree in economics and a master's in public administration.

Jamil Salmi, a Moroccan education economist, is the World Bank's tertiary education coordinator. He is the principal author of the Bank's tertiary education strategy, titled "Constructing Knowledge Societies: New Challenges for Tertiary Education." In the past 17 years, Salmi has provided policy and technical advice on tertiary education reform to the governments of more than 60 countries in Europe, Asia, Africa, and South America. Salmi is a member of the Governing Board of the International Institute for Educational Planning, the International Rankings Expert Group, the International Advisory Network of the UK Leadership Foundation for Higher Education, and the Editorial Committee of OECD's *Journal of Higher Education Management and Policy*. Salmi's latest book, published in February 2009, is *The Challenge of Establishing World-Class Universities*.

Spencer Witte is a policy analyst and researcher for Ishtirak, a MENA-focused consultancy. Prior to joining Ishtirak, he was a freelance journalist, reporting from Beirut during the 2006 Lebanon-Israel war. Most recently, Witte has written for The Observatory on Borderless Higher Education and *International Higher Education*. He holds a BA in history from the University of Pennsylvania and an MPhil in modern Middle Eastern studies from St. Antony's College, University of Oxford. His master's dissertation was titled *Higher Education in the Gulf: America's Universities in Qatar and the UAE*.

John L. Yeager is an associate professor in the Administrative and Policy Studies Program in the School of Education at the University of Pittsburgh, in addition to serving as director of the Institute for Higher Education Management. He has held several senior university administrative posts such as vice chancellor for administration and vice chancellor for planning and budget, as well as department positions. He has consulted and conducted in service programs on a number of management subjects and in the development of strategic plans both in the United States and internationally. He currently teaches courses on institutional strategic planning, university finance, human resource management, and program quality. He has worked in several counties including Mongolia, Kenya, China, Thailand, and South Africa. His major current interests are focused on international strategic planning and quality assurance practices. Yeager has published numerous papers, made professional presentations, and conducted workshops.

IIE Information and Resources

OPEN DOORS REPORT ON INTERNATIONAL EDUCATIONAL EXCHANGE

The Open Doors Report on International Educational Exchange, supported by the U.S. Department of State, Bureau of Educational and Cultural Affairs, provides an annual, comprehensive statistical analysis of academic mobility between the United States and other nations, and trend data over 60 years.

WEBSITE: www.opendoors.iienetwork.org

THE CENTER FOR INTERNATIONAL PARTNERSHIPS IN HIGHER EDUCATION

The IIE Center for International Partnerships in Higher Education assists colleges and universities in developing and sustaining institutional partnerships with their counterparts around the world. A major initiative of the Center is the International Academic Partnerships Program, funded by the U.S. Department of Education's Fund for the Improvement of Postsecondary Education (FIPSE).

EMAIL: iapp@iie.org

ATLAS OF STUDENT MOBILITY

Project Atlas tracks migration trends of the millions of students who pursue education outside of their home countries each year. Data are collected on global student mobility patterns, country of origin, as well as leading host destinations for higher education.

WEBSITE: http://atlas.iienetwork.org

IIE STUDY ABROAD WHITE PAPER SERIES: MEETING AMERICA'S GLOBAL EDUCATION CHALLENGE

An IIE policy research initiative that addresses the issue of increasing capacity in the U.S. and abroad, in order to help pave the way for substantial study abroad growth.

- Expanding Study Abroad Capacity at U.S. Colleges and Universities (May 2009)
- Promoting Study Abroad in Science and Technology Fields (March 2009)
- Expanding U.S. Study Abroad in the Arab World: Challenges & Opportunities (February 2009)
- Expanding Education Abroad at Community Colleges (September 2008)
- Exploring Host Country Capacity for Increasing U.S. Study Abroad (May 2008)
- Current Trends in U.S. Study Abroad & the Impact of Strategic Diversity Initiatives(May 2007)

WEBSITE: www.iie.org/StudyAbroadCapacity

IIE/AIFS FOUNDATION GLOBAL EDUCATION RESEARCH REPORTS

This series explores the most pressing and under-researched issues affecting international education policy today.

- Innovation through Education: Building the Knowledge Economy in the Middle East (May 2010)
- International India: A Turning Point in Educational Exchange with the U.S. (January 2010)
- Higher Education on the Move: New Developments in Global Mobility (April 2009)
- U.S.-China Educational Exchange: Perspectives on a Growing Partnership (October 2008)

IIE BRIEFING PAPERS

IIE Briefing Papers are a rapid response to the changing landscape of international education, offering timely snapshots of critical issues in the field.

- Attitudes and Perceptions of Prospective International Students from Vietnam (January 2010)
- Attitudes and Perceptions of Prospective International Students from India (December 2009)
- The Value of International Education to U.S. Business and Industry Leaders: Key Findings from a Survey of CEOs (October 2009)
- The Three-year Bologna-compliant Degree: Responses from U.S. Graduate Schools (April 2009)
- Educational Exchange between the United States and China (July 2008)

WEBSITE: www.iie.org/researchpublications

IIE Web Resources

IIEPASSPORT.ORG

This free online search engine lists over 9,000 study abroad programs worldwide and provides advisers with hands-on tools to counsel students and promote study abroad.

WEBSITE: www.iiepassport.org

STUDY ABROAD FUNDING

This valuable funding resource helps U.S. students find funding for their study abroad.

WEBSITE: www.studyabroadfunding.org

FUNDING FOR UNITED STATES STUDY

This directory offers the most relevant data on hundreds of fellowships, grants, paid internships and scholarships for study in the U.S.

WEBSITE: www.fundingusstudy.org

INTENSIVE ENGLISH USA

Comprehensive reference with over 500 accredited English language programs in the U.S.

WEBSITE: www.intensiveenglishusa.org

IIE RESOURCES FOR STUDY ABROAD

IIE offers a single point of entry to access valuable study abroad information, including policy research, data on study abroad trends, news coverage of new developments, fact sheets for students, and dates and deadlines for major scholarship and fellowship programs.

WEBSITE: www.iie.org/studyabroad

INTERNATIONALIZING THE CAMPUS

IIE administers a wealth of programs and provides a variety of services and resources to help U.S. colleges and universities develop and implement their strategies for greater campus internationalization.

WEBSITE: www.iie.org/internationalizing

FULBRIGHT PROGRAMS FOR U.S. STUDENTS

The Fulbright U.S. Student Program equips future American leaders with the skills they need to thrive in an increasingly global environment by providing funding for one academic year of study or research abroad, to be conducted after gradu¬ation from an accredited university.

SPONSOR: U.S. Department of State, Bureau of Educational and Cultural Affairs

WEBSITE: http://us.fulbrightonline.org

FULBRIGHT PROGRAMS FOR U.S. SCHOLARS

The traditional Fulbright Scholar Program sends 800 U.S. faculty and professionals abroad each year. Grantees lecture and conduct research in a wide variety of academic and professional fields.

SPONSOR: U.S. Department of State, Bureau of Educational and Cultural Affairs

WEBSITE: www.cies.org

Programs of the AIFS Foundation

The AIFS Foundation

The mission of the AIFS Foundation is to provide educational and cultural exchange opportunities to foster greater understanding among the people of the world. It seeks to fulfill this mission by organizing high quality educational opportunities for students, and providing grants to individuals and schools for participation in culturally enriching educational programs.

WEBSITE: www.aifsfoundation.org

ACADEMIC YEAR IN AMERICA

Each year, AYA brings nearly 1,000 high school students from around the world to the United States. They come for the school year, to live with American families and attend local high schools, learning about American culture and sharing their own languages and customs with their host families.

WEBSITE: www.academicyear.org

FUTURE LEADERS EXCHANGE PROGRAM (FLEX)

Established in 1992 under the FREEDOM Support Act and administered by the U.S. Department of State's Bureau of Educational and Cultural Affairs, FLEX encourages long-lasting peace and mutual understanding between the U.S. and countries of Eurasia.

YOUTH EXCHANGE AND STUDY PROGRAM (YES)

Since 2002, this U.S. Department of State high school exchange program has enabled students from predominantly Muslim countries to learn about American society and values, acquire leadership skills, and help educate Americans about their countries and cultures.

Programs of the American Institute For Foreign Study

The American Institute For Foreign Study

The AIFS mission is to enrich the lives of young people throughout the world by providing them with educational and cultural exchange programs of the highest possible quality.

WEBSITE: www.aifs.com

AIFS COLLEGE STUDY ABROAD

AIFS is a leading provider of study abroad programs for college students. Students can study abroad for a summer, semester or academic year in 17 countries around the world.

WEBSITE: www.aifsabroad.com

AIFS INTERNATIONAL STUDENT RECRUITMENT SERVICES

With a worldwide network of staff and partners, AIFS is working to recruit and screen international students and guide them through the American university admissions process, to assist U.S. institutions with developing a more diverse student population.

WEBSITE: www.aifsrecruitment.com

AIFS SUMMER ADVANTAGE

Based on the AIFS College Division programs, AIFS Summer Advantage offers high school students age 16 and older the opportunity to earn college credits while studying overseas during the summer.

WEBSITE: www.summeradvantage.com

AIFS UNIVERSITY PREP

High school sophomores and juniors learn the ins and outs of the American university admissions process, making them strong and polished applicants. Students spend three weeks taking courses in SAT prep that are designed to raise scores significantly, practicing college admissions strategies, and touring area colleges.

WEBSITE: www.aifsuniversityprep.com

AMERICAN COUNCIL FOR INTERNATIONAL STUDIES (ACIS)

For more than 30 years, ACIS has helped students and their teachers discover the world through premier travel and education. Teachers can choose destinations throughout Europe, the Americas, and Asiaaround the world to experience with their students, throughout Europe, the Americas and Asia.

WEBSITE: www.acis.com

AU PAIR IN AMERICA

Au Pair in America makes it possible for nearly 4,000 eager and skilled young adults from around the world to join American families and help care for their children during a mutually rewarding, year--long cultural exchange experience.

WEBSITE: www.aupairinamerica.com

CAMP AMERICA AND RESORT AMERICA

Each summer, Camp America and Resort America bring nearly 8,000 young people from around the world to the U.S. to work as camp counselors and resort staff.

WEBSITE: www.campamerica.aifs.com

SUMMER INSTITUTE FOR THE GIFTED (SIG)

SIG is a three- week academic, recreational and social summer program for gifted and talented students. Students from around the world in grades 4 through 11 can participate in SIG Residential programs offered at university campuses across the country including Dartmouth, Princeton, and UC Berkeley.

WEBSITE: www.giftedstudy.org